Praise for Pawprints On Our Hearts

2022 Royal Dragonfly 4x Book Award Winner
2022 The BookFest 3x Award Winner
2022 Reader's Favorite Book Award Winner
2022 Reader's Choice Book Award Finalist

"Animal lovers will feel connected to Murray's almost spiritual awakening and admire his devotion to following his heart, even in the face of tremendous sacrifice. This touching memoir overflows with intense emotion."

— Booklife by Publishers Weekly

"The author is a natural storyteller, so much so that although this is his first book, he has complete control of his style and story."

— Readers' Favorite

"A deeply moving memoir... one of the best books that capture the connection between human beings and dogs... Pawprints on Our Hearts inspires a love for animals while exploring the painful edges of the human in need of love and healing."

— The Book Commentary

"A powerful and emotional story."
— Alyson Sheldrake, Bestselling author of
"Kat the Dog"

"Heartfelt... Whether you love dogs or not, you'll enjoy this book and learn much from it."
— R. Janet Walraven, Award winning author
of "Rainbow of Promise"

"There is so much hope, courage and love poured into these pages and I am so thankful this found its way to me. It's one of my 2022 favorites and one I highly recommend."
— Reader Review

"This is a book I will continue to recommend to others and I can see me going back and reading it again and again."
— Reader Review

"It draws you in on such a deep level, touching chords that we can all connect to, moments and memories that we've all experienced in our own lives."

— Reader Review

"I never leave reviews but I had to after reading this sweet book. This book was so good. Had me laughing and crying."

— Reader Review

"This is such a beautifully written personal story of the author and the impact dogs have had on his life, the joy and love they brought."

— Reader Review

KERK
MURRAY
Sun, Sand, and Sweet Romance

BY KERK MURRAY

Pawprints On Our Hearts
Since the Day We Danced
Since the Day We Fell
Since the Day We Kissed
Since the Day We Wished
Since the Day We Left
Since the Day We Promised

Pawprints
On Our Hearts

How A Few Incredible Dogs
Changed One Life Forever

KERK MURRAY

To all the animals who were forced to endure
cruelty in the hands of evildoers. Your innocence
will never be forgotten—this one's for you.

Maximus

Spartacus

Before You Begin...

You're invited to join my private Facebook Reader Group, where you'll make new book friends, meet other animal lovers, and be the first to know about new releases, book clubs, and special deals.

Join now:
Kerk Murray's private Facebook Reader Group
facebook.com/groups/779562103953550

Contents

"Love of animals is a universal impulse,
a common ground on which all of us
may meet. By loving and understanding
animals, perhaps we humans shall
come to understand each other."
— Louis J. Camuti

Dear Reader,

We often remember the story of our lives as a blur of a million moments, sloppily compiled into the scrapbook of our minds. As the days become months and those months become years, the details of these moments slowly fade away and are buried in some distant place that even the most skilled cartographer would never find. But among the blur are those few defining moments we could never forget—some that made us smile, and others that made us cry. Whether it's the nostalgia of a childhood Christmas morning or the trauma endured while we held an animal we loved as they took their last breath, these moments have the power to change us from who we are into who we're meant to be.

When I recall the defining moments in my life, I can't help but think of the animals who changed me.

This may surprise some of you, but I wasn't always the animal lover I am today. For the longest time, I thought caring for animals was just another responsibility of humankind, an act that only benefited the animals. Looking back, I couldn't have been more wrong. Today, I believe God desires for us to extend compassion to all animals, but not solely for us to change their lives. I suspect His principal reasoning is for these animals to change us—that their capacity to love and be loved may one day awaken the possibilities living within us all.

I've read touching stories highlighting the powerful bond between humans and animals ranging from cats, dogs, horses, goats, pigs, chickens, and even snakes.

Although I love all animals, my experiences have always been with dogs—Chelsea, Lexi, Maximus, Spartacus, and Gunner, to name them all.

In this book, I unpack my life's journey alongside these incredible dogs, whose immeasurable impact led me to founding a nonprofit organization that advocates for animal welfare. I'm neither a natural writer nor an orator. I'm nobody special—just a guy with a story who learned about love, friendship, and forgiveness from some unlikely heroes. I say "unlikely" because, at the end of the day, they're dogs—they slobber, chew up shoes, and poop on your new hardwood floors even after you've taken them outside. But there's something more to these intricate beings that draws us closely together—a force that exists in an invisible realm beyond the grasp of our understanding. It's a phenomenon that isn't easily explained, yet it's undeniably felt. There's little in our human experience that compares to the joys of loving and being loved by an animal.

Whether your animal companion is still with you or has passed, I hope as you read my story you'll envision yourself in your own story and recall those defining moments that changed you. And afterward, you'll arrive at this inexorable truth: as much as your beloved animal needed you, you also needed them.

C. S. Lewis writes to his goddaughter Lucy in his dedication of *The Lion, the Witch, and the Wardrobe,*

"Someday you will be old enough to start reading fairy tales again."

For reasons beyond my understanding, I've been fortunate enough to have lived my own fairy tale. It's altogether ugly and beautiful, sorrowful and hilarious, fearful and courageous, despairing and redeeming. Despite life being painful at times, I wouldn't have had it any other way. It's made me who I am today—flaws and all. Although I've been alive for thirty-three years, I'm realizing that my story has just begun. And with some help from these beautiful creatures, both those of my past and present, I'm slowly discovering who I'm meant to be.

I wish for the day to arrive when you'll bravely embrace your own fairy tale that was lived alongside the animals in your life—with all of its joys, sorrows, love, and loss. And in that moment, you'll truly understand that these animals live within us forever—leaving behind their pawprints on our hearts.

Your friend,

Kerk

Part 1
A Daring Adventure

"Life is either a daring adventure or nothing at all."

—Helen Keller

Chapter 1
The Living Room Wall

On the morning of March 15, 2020, it was still dark outside when I pulled the covers over my head, as if it would somehow deafen me to the echoes of reverberating barks throughout the house. It was the familiar sound of our dogs, Maximus and Spartacus, engaging in their morning ritual. I suppose this early morning barking was their way of letting us know it was time to get up. Or, better yet, it was their way of disregarding our attempt to sleep in after checking off several items from the never-ending list of to-dos after a long workweek.

Maximus is a thirteen-pound, dark-haired Yorkie-poo with an attitude, but he has moments when he can be sweet. His counterpart, Spartacus, is a thirteen-pound, white and copper Morkie—a peacemaker—who mostly follows Maximus's lead. While their statures are small, their persistence is not. My wife, Crystal, and I tried our best to ignore them, but as we lay there, the decibel levels of the barking only intensified.

This is a normal occurrence for us.

There was nothing special about this day, except that it was Sunday—the one morning I looked forward to all week, mostly because it didn't require me to set an alarm. Yet, here we were, all at once exhausted, but fully alert, resisting the demands of our four-legged furry companions. It was a battle of wills we were convinced we'd win if we could do one thing: simply wait it out.

I slowly rolled over to squint at the alarm clock—as if I would have been able to see it. It was only sitting a few feet from me, but my vision is so poor that I couldn't see what time it was without my glasses. I surprise myself each morning because I always seem to forget this fact. As I reached over for my glasses, I found myself disappointed once again. They were on the nightstand; but about two inches out of my grasp.

Frustrated, I thought to myself, *Dammit! I'm too blind to see but too tired to get up.*

I rolled back over and put my arm around Crystal. It didn't take long for us to realize that the fortifications of our human will were no match for the siege of our dogs' barks. Their constant barrage of high-pitched yelps forced us to wave the white flag of surrender. After fully accepting defeat, Crystal and I both stared at each other, eyes half-open, wondering the same thing.

Are you gonna let them out?

We both paused, waiting for the other to budge. Usually Crystal would concede first if I lay there long enough, but that day, something overcame me, quickly forcing me up and out of bed. It was my bladder screaming at me to find the nearest toilet—and by some miracle, I made it just in time.

Stumbling out of the bathroom, barely holding my eyes open, I fought the temptation to lie back down.

"Well hell, I'm already up. Might as well get the day started," I grumbled to myself, but not silently enough.

"What was that?" Crystal mumbled.

Surprised that she'd heard me, I responded, "Nothing at all. I suppose I'll get the boys ready this morning."

"It's about time you do something around here," she said, half-joking.

I laughed, acknowledging the truth in her statement, and walked out of the bedroom, shutting the door behind me. As I headed down the hall toward the kitchen, their barking ceased. The very moment they saw me, Maximus and Spartacus sprinted toward me with a familiar excitement that never fails to make me smile. Even though it's only been a handful of hours since they last saw me, I was greeted like a long-lost friend they hadn't seen in years.

Still half-asleep, I squatted down to embrace them as they jumped all over me and smothered me with their kisses. Unable to contain their joy, they ended up scratching me—as usual. Forget coffee; there's nothing like getting clawed by an animal early in the morning to completely wake you up.

With every bit of willpower left in me, I restrained myself from cursing—a vice I've tried to eliminate over the years, although I still slip up every now and then.

"Dang it, boys! Watch your nails. That freaking' hurt!"

I knew they meant well, and I wasn't really mad at them. It was just a knee-jerk reaction to the pain. If anything, I should've been grateful that they help me practice self-control.

But that morning, they didn't just scratch me. Their paws found an old tear on my favorite pajamas I was wearing, and they had made the tear even larger.

I let out a sigh. "Why am I even surprised?"

Noticing the severity of the rip, I doubted these pajamas could be saved—hell, the left pant leg was barely hanging on. I began to wonder if I could find another pair that I'd love just as much. It's funny to think I had become so attached to a pair of Budweiser pajamas, considering I hate beer, but they were just so comfortable.

When the dogs finally calmed down, I held together what was left of my favorite pajamas and headed toward the kitchen to cook their breakfast. As strange as that may sound, we do cook meals for our dogs—even though we rarely cook for ourselves—and they think we're the best chefs in the world. By simply combining peanut butter with beans, rice, and blueberries, they're as happy as can be.

As the stove was heating, the familiar sound of coconut oil sizzling in the pan got them excited once again. They paced hastily back and forth, paws pattering on the kitchen tile, knowing it was almost time to eat. While their food was cooking, I took a moment to make myself some tea in the microwave. I grabbed an old mug from the cupboard printed with faded text, "Enjoy the little things"—a reminder to love the present moment so I don't miss out on the real treasures of life.

When the kitchen timer went off, I grabbed their bowls and set them on the counter. The scraping of the spoon against the pan as I filled their bowls really got their attention. Anticipating their upcoming meal, they began jumping around and all over me, as if they hadn't had food in days.

In my attempt to take control of the situation, I gave them the command, "Sit, boys. Sit."

They rarely ever listen the first time, and that day was no exception. I had to say it once again but differently. This time, I took a deep breath and held it out a little longer.

"Siiiiiit."

As they sat in complete obedience, a false sense of confidence came over me. I felt just as capable of training dogs as Caesar Milan, the famed Dog Whisperer.

"Good boys, good boys," I reaffirmed, careful to use positive reinforcement.

Feeling satisfied with their compliance and in myself as the new unofficial Dog Whisperer, I rewarded them by placing their food bowls on the kitchen floor. Maximus and Spartacus spared no time reconnecting with their wolf ancestry, ravaging the food as if it were the spoils from their hunt in the wild.

Though, let's face the facts: they wouldn't survive a day out in the wilderness, despite the ferocity they display during feeding time.

We have to supervise them during this daily event. Maximus always finishes his food first and often finds himself slowly creeping toward Spartacus's bowl. He appears innocent but really is waiting for his opportunity to get more than his fair share. Although this has caused some issues between the dogs in the past, it's been easily corrected with some coaching.

"No, no, Maximus."

Most of the time he listens, even when I use a tone that sounds like he's being rewarded rather than reprimanded. My wife often reminds me of this, telling me to be more firm with him.

The thing is, Spartacus won't stand his ground. He's just a kind, down-to-earth homebody. A pacifist, even to his own detriment. Maximus, on the other hand, is also kind, but mischievous. He's always ready to push the limits of any boundaries. If we've learned anything from them, it's that they're two different individuals—and we treat them as such.

After Spartacus finished eating, I grabbed my tea from the microwave and opened the back door to let them run in the yard. Leaning against the door frame, I inhaled the wonderful scent of my peppermint tea, slowly sipping and watching them play. The steam from the mug dissipated into the air, but the scent of peppermint continued to linger, initiating a sense of gratitude for all simple pleasures in life.

It was just past seven in the morning, the perfect time to witness a spring sunrise over the South Georgia horizon. Beams of sunshine peeked through the gaps in our fence as they magnified the morning mist on the grass. The dogs were chasing each other and prancing around without a worry in the world, the dew splashing on them. I couldn't help but smile.

Upon glancing back inside, I looked at what was hanging on the living room wall, which caused me to pause in reverence. It's a hand-painted portrait of Maximus and Spartacus. To the left of it hangs Lexi's pink bandanna along with Chelsea's green collar. And to the right is a photo of me holding Gunner the day I rescued him. All of these things—the portrait, the bandanna, the collar, and the photo—are reminders of the brevity of life.

More often than not, I'm overwhelmed with emotions when I look at what's hanging on the living room wall. It captures what has passed and what cannot be again—this fact is a hard pill to swallow. Some days, I'll look at the wall and smile, thinking of all the wonderful moments we shared together. But other days, I break down and sob uncontrollably. In those distressing moments, one particular line from *Brushstrokes of a Gadfly*, a novel written by E. A. Bucchianeri, resonates so deeply: "So it's true, when all is said and done, grief is the price we pay for love."

Although it's painful to view at times, those things that hang on the wall force me to slow down and consider what's really important in life. I've wasted countless years chasing things that ultimately didn't matter. But life will always find ways to compel us so we can be still and look up from its distractions for even a moment. This is what it takes for us to leave behind who we are so we can arrive at who we're meant to be.

What I've discovered matters most to me in life has certainly changed over the years. I've lost all ambition toward the empty pursuits of money, status, and approval. Alternatively, I want nothing more than to become a person who views others through the lens of compassion. To guide me, I've adopted this lyric by the late River Phoenix as my life mantra: "Run to the rescue with love, and peace will follow."

That's what these dogs did for me, and it's what I set out to do for all living beings—humans and animals. I often fall short of exemplifying this lyric and realize I have much to learn about love from these beautiful creatures.

Perhaps I was mistaken earlier when I claimed there was nothing special about that particular March day; for that was the day I finally picked up a pen to write the fairy tale I lived alongside these incredible dogs—the ones who changed me forever and left their pawprints on my heart.

Chapter 2

"Trust Me."

One of my earliest experiences with a dog was certainly memorable, but not in the sense that it would merit a celebratory Facebook post. In fact, it was memorable in the same vein as a high school breakup—it was painful then, but you can laugh about it now. And you laugh at the fact that it actually surprised you, even though, in retrospect, every sign indicated it would never work out.

My experience with this particular dog was similar—I should've seen trouble on the horizon. In hindsight, it wasn't the dog's fault at all—it was mine.

Although two decades have passed since this incident, I can recall it as if it were yesterday.

The event took place during another scorching Georgia summer back in July of 2000. My good friend Colt and I were doing what middle school boys do for entertainment—getting into trouble. Back then, we didn't have the distractions of the iPhone or social media. At that time, we were raving about AOL dial-up, AIM instant messenger, and Nextel's push-to-talk phones—those things were life back then.

Doubled-over, trying to catch my breath, I could barely speak. "Dude, I can't believe we got away with that!"

"Yeah! That was so damn crazy," Colt replied.

Colt and I were ding dong ditching around local neighborhoods in broad daylight. The rush of sneaking up on some poor sap's door, ringing the bell, disturbing them from whatever they may be doing, and running as fast as we could was strangely euphoric.

"You wanna do another one?" Colt asked.

"Hell yeah," I answered, exuding bravado, thinking I was a total badass.

In reality, my thirteen-year-old delusional self was far from being an alpha male. At five foot eight, just shy of weighing one hundred and ten pounds, and rocking a comb over with way too much gel, I apparently looked like a "wet bird," according to my mom. (To all the girls who turned me down that year, I don't blame you. I completely get it—I really do.)

Colt and I had a method to our madness; we didn't just ding dong ditch random houses. There was surveillance done on our end. Our version of intelligence gathering was creepily circling cul-de-sacs, pretending we were just some innocent kids walking around.

"All right, I think this is the one," I confidently stated, nodding my head at the white colonial-style house with blue shutters and a wrap-around porch.

"I dunno, bro. There's like four cars parked in their driveway."

"So?"

"Dude, a lot of people live there. We'll definitely get caught."

"Bro, stop being such a baby. We won't get caught. Trust me," I reassured him with raised brows.

Arms crossed, he stood his ground. "You know what? I'm not going up there man, you can go by yourself."

"All right, watch me," I scoffed.

Colt distanced himself and hid behind a hill in someone's yard as I slowly approached this stranger's front door. We had done this so many times that day, but my intuition was sensing something unusual about this episode of ding dong ditch. I wasn't sure what, but whatever it was, I definitely wasn't backing out now. Plus, if I did this and got away with it, I could hold it over Colt's head for a while, which was the ultimate depth of kinship any middle school boy could wish to have with his best friend. In our quest to become men, we proudly boasted our courageous deeds over one another—but in this case, it wasn't courage as much as it was stupidity.

As I stepped closer to the door, doubt overtook me. I wondered about those four cars and who could be inside that house. We'd never been caught before, but I couldn't stop wondering if I should've listened to Colt.

Standing on the welcome mat, my attention was drawn to the fine craftsmanship of the oak rocking chair, moving ever so slightly in the breeze. The wind chimes clinked together eerily. Time slowed down, yet my heart raced.

With sweat beading across my brow, I finally gathered myself and reached up to ring the doorbell. Before I could press the button, the sudden turning of the knob stopped me. Frozen in fear, I knew this wasn't good news. The door burst wide open, and I nearly shat myself. Colt was right.

A humongous Doberman pinscher, unleashed and growling, suddenly stood within biting distance. The dog looked just as surprised as I did, but didn't hesitate to remind me that I was in danger, snapping at me with ear-piercing barks.

Startled, I stepped backward and tripped over a potted plant. I jumped back up and started sprinting for dear life. I faintly heard the lady shout from the front door as I bolted off of her lawn, "Get off my damn yard!"

She was the least of my concerns. When I finally made it to the hill where Colt was hiding, I could tell something was terribly wrong with one look into his eyes. I glanced behind me to see what was causing Colt's distress and there it was—that dog was in a full sprint, closing in on both of us!

"Oh, shit!"

My adrenaline was in overdrive as I kept running. Out of self-preservation, Colt sprinted in the opposite direction, fleeing for his life. Like a flash grenade, the Doberman's barks were nearly deafening and reinforced my primal fear. I could feel hot breath against my legs as the dog attempted to bite me, barely missing my calves each time—it was that close. Stopping was not an option, as I'd have no chance of defending myself against this beast, who visibly outweighed me both in mass and ferocity.

After half a mile, I could feel my adrenaline wearing off and knew I couldn't go much longer. Even being fully aware of the consequences if I were to stop running, my body couldn't sustain this pace. Realizing this, I resigned myself from outrunning the dog to just surviving an attack. For a moment, I really believed this was it for me, and I would soon be meeting my Creator, which threw me into a mental panic.

I haven't even been laid yet. I'm gonna die a virgin!

(Yes, those were my thirteen-year-old mind's concerns when facing death.)

As my sprinting slowed to a jog, I advised myself, Just don't let the dog bite your neck.

But, to my surprise, I couldn't feel the impending doom anymore—yet I wasn't quite ready to trust my judgment again (the same judgment that got me into this mess).

When my body was on the brink of giving out, I turned my head and looked over my shoulder for a split second. To my relief, the dog wasn't chasing me anymore. I stopped and fell to the ground, attempting to catch my breath.

Barely escaping death, and lying in some stranger's yard, I came to realize how much I appreciated the softness of fresh cut grass. Rolling over, I noticed the Doberman was in the yard across from me, only forty feet away staring in my direction. I was no longer concerned for my safety, seeing his calm demeanor as he sat, licking his balls completely unashamed. I wondered if he had forgotten the entire episode. I surely didn't. Although I felt in the clear, I made sure to keep my eye on him in case he changed his mind. Eventually he wandered off and out of my sight, which brought tremendous relief.

That night, I thanked God for sparing my life. I didn't even bother asking Him for anything like I usually did. Back then, my prayer life only existed during emergencies or when I wanted something. I thought of God as some sort of genie whose purpose was to fulfill my personal wish list—a real-life Santa Claus. Hoping to get my prayers answered, I'd barter with God, making empty promises on things I never followed through on.

For example, "God, I know I didn't study, but if you can score me an A on my science test, I promise I won't cuss for a week, and I'll stop staring at Christina Aguilera's butt whenever her new music video plays on TRL. Just help me this one time, God. Please. Amen."

Although I truly believed the good Lord saved my life that day, it wasn't enough to make me more intentional in my prayers. But the fact that I had survived this incident certainly made me ponder the purpose of my existence and the value of my life.

Why did God save me? Would He ever do it again?

At thirteen, the smallness of my thinking regarding the identity of God was naïve at best.

In his book, *Tattoos on the Heart*, Gregory Boyle stirs our wonder with this truth, "How much greater is the God we have than the one we think we have."

That day was the last time I ever played ding dong ditch, and I never traveled through that same neighborhood again, for any reason whatsoever. Now that I was officially terrified of dogs, I avoided them like the plague, wanting absolutely nothing to do with them. But life certainly didn't care about my fear of canines. And looking back, I'm glad it didn't.

Chapter 3
An Unlikely Friend

The next month, August of 2000, I ate lunch alone in the bathroom during my first day of eighth grade. It wasn't as bad as it sounds—actually it was peaceful until some other kids started throwing wet paper towels over the stall. They caught me off-guard and totally defenseless. Those bombs were hard to dodge while sitting on a toilet seat and clinging onto my lunch tray as if it were the last meal I'd ever eat. I'm not sure how those kids had my exact coordinates, but they hit me on every attempt.

Eventually, they called a ceasefire and left. The water from the paper towels ran down my hair and face as I gathered up what dignity remained and opened the stall door. I stepped out, walking toward the mirror, and placed my lunch tray on the counter near the sink. As I leaned in to wash my face, I noticed a piece of white paper towel had broken off onto my head. This alarmed me. Something was wrong—very wrong.

Why is this white paper towel now yellow?

With a brief investigation, I discovered they had dipped the paper towels into the piss-filled urinal before throwing them at me. Disgusted and embarrassed, I vigorously washed my hair and face with the hand soap, nearly emptying the entire dispenser. Afterward, I squatted down awkwardly, attempting to use the hand dryer on my wet hair. The bell rang, not leaving enough time to completely dry myself. I hurried, picking up my bag and scarfing down what was left of my lunch before scurrying back to class.

Despite the unforgettable bathroom lunch, the rest of the day went well, and I made new friends—some that I've remained in contact with to this day. Years before, the thought of socializing had given me anxiety due to a lack of self-confidence from being labeled a four-eyed Asian nerd.

But eighth grade proved to be a transition year in my life. It was the first year I started wearing contacts and was no longer called "four eyes." Even more importantly, an unlikely friend changed my life forever.

I remember the day I met her. My mom brought her home as a gift from one of her clients. Her name was Chelsea, a ten-year-old miniature pinscher rescued from an abusive situation. She wasn't the cuddly, fun-loving dog you imagine your parents bringing home—she was grumpy, hostile, and definitely didn't want to cuddle. Although Chelsea was small in stature, I was still fearful of her unpredictable aggression. This fear was amplified by what had happened to me the previous month, barely surviving a Doberman attack.

We also found it very odd that she shared the same name as my sister—but we never bothered to change it. We thought changing her name would only confuse the senior canine. Instead, the entire family remained confused for the duration of the dog's life.

Someone would ask, "Where's Chelsea?"

And without fail, they'd get the same response that would be repeated for years: "Which one?"

The first night we had Chelsea, she sat under the table while we were having dinner—leftover spaghetti, a typical dish for our family. And when I say "typical," I mean on Sundays, my mom would cook a huge, Costco-sized batch, and we'd eat it the next week—every day for dinner.

As Chelsea found her place in front of my chair, sitting near my foot, she began growling incessantly with all thirteen pounds of her being. Here we were, doing Chelsea a favor by bringing her into our home and all she could do was act out—how dare she? My thirteen-year-old self just didn't have the capacity to comprehend that her present behaviors were the effects of her past trauma. It's not my fault she had a bad life. She should be grateful to be here. Back then those were my thoughts, and ultimately the measure of my compassion.

I attempted to eat but was too distracted by her snarls that got even louder as she laid next to my feet. These sounds frightened me, and fearing she was going to bite, I slammed my fork down, snapping back at her, "If you bite me, I'll kill you!"

To my relief, Chelsea stopped growling, cowering on the cold kitchen tile in complete silence. But what I hadn't noticed right away was that everyone at the dinner table was staring at me, in shock that I could say such a thing.

Despite my threats, I never could've followed through with intentionally harming an animal.

Although my words didn't affect me then as a thirteen-year-old, twenty years later I cringe when I think of that moment, disgusted at my lack of empathy. Chelsea certainly arrived with a ton of baggage and like any of us, what she needed was compassion, not judgment.

In her book, *The Candymakers*, Wendy Mass writes, "Be kind, for everyone you meet is fighting a battle you know nothing about."

Through Chelsea, I learned this is just as true for animals as it is for humans. Some say that "time heals all wounds." But I don't agree with that well-intentioned sentiment. Through the years, I've come to believe that some traumas in life are just carried and made only lighter through compassion, as in Chelsea's case.

As dinner went on that night, I almost forgot Chelsea was sitting by my foot. She had mellowed out, tired from all the growling she had done. Glancing down, I noticed she was fast asleep.

My heart melted. She looked so precious. It was a sweet moment that made me realize she was experiencing what we all desire—a safe place to call home.

After I finished eating, I got up from my chair, which woke Chelsea. But she didn't bite me. She didn't even growl. She just gave me a strange look and closed her eyes once again. I left the table unscathed, a far cry from my expectations at the beginning of dinner. Looking back, I doubt it was Chelsea's intention to bite me that night. She simply was voicing her boundaries, ones that had been violated in her life before us.

Our first dinner with Chelsea helped me connect the dots between the shared experiences of humans and animals. For the first time in my life, I realized animals had the capacity to feel love, joy, fear, and could certainly suffer. When I viewed Chelsea through that lens, it was clear to me we weren't much different—she was *someone,* not something.

Chapter 4

"Bad Dog!"

Over the last few weeks of that summer, Chelsea and I spent time learning about each other. One weekend afternoon, we were sitting on separate sides of an old sofa upstairs, watching TV, and dozing off for a nap. I sat with my eyes closed for several minutes, unable to fall asleep. The TV was just a few decibels too loud for me, but Chelsea's snores told me it didn't bother her at all. I needed to turn the volume down, but Chelsea was lying on the remote control.

I considered the alternative of standing up, walking to the TV, and using its buttons, but I was way too comfortable to do all of that. Holding my breath, I leaned over to where Chelsea was fast asleep and slowly crept my hand toward the remote. Once I gripped it, going at a snail's pace, I carefully pulled the remote out from underneath her leg, so as not to wake her. But I wasn't careful enough. Startled, she swiftly turned in my direction and let out a menacing snarl that made the hair on the back of my neck stand up, before snapping at me, nearly biting my hand.

The adrenaline pumped through my veins as her reaction took me aback.

What the hell!?

Chelsea scrambled off the couch and dashed across the beige carpet to an empty corner. Curious and a bit confused, I got up and followed her. When she heard me, she stopped, turned around, and looked me right in the eyes, as if she were trying to tell me something. And that's when she did it; she squatted and took a major dump all over the carpet.

Shocked, I stood statuesque in disbelief at how much shit that little dog pushed out.

Chelsea wasn't ashamed of this at all. After christening the carpet with her turds, she trotted back over toward the couch, hopping on, and laid back down on the remote as if nothing had ever happened. For me, there was no more relaxing to be done—I had a mess to clean up. But I wasn't angry with her. I chalked it up to an accident, given she was a senior dog.

From that day on, I vowed to take Chelsea outside before her afternoon naps so there wouldn't be any more accidents. Furthermore, I made it a point to not disturb her while she was sleeping, for any reason whatsoever. I also found out that laminate floors were much easier to clean than carpet.

A few nights later, during one of my mom's famous leftover spaghetti dinners, the doorbell rang. It was a neighborhood kid and their parents selling candy for a school fundraiser. My parents made small talk with the other adults as my siblings and I were distracted, enamored with the possibility of a sugar rush with all the options displayed in front of us. I could almost taste the sweetness of the white chocolate...

That's when we heard silverware clanking on the kitchen floor.

My mom abruptly broke off the meeting with our neighbors—and without candy, to our dismay—immediately hustling back to the kitchen.

In that moment of our absence, we discovered that our thirteen-pound senior dog was an acrobat. Chelsea was standing on the table, devouring our dinner, unabashed. She looked at us proudly with spaghetti sauce on her nose and a loaf of bread in her mouth. I glanced at my mom, who was furious as she stood with widened eyes and clenched fists. I fought hard, biting my lip to hold back laughter—I don't think I'd ever heard her yell so loud.

"Bad dog!"

Chelsea knew she was in trouble, leaping off the table onto the chair, then back onto the kitchen floor. She scurried away with the loot in her mouth, leaving behind a trail of splattered spaghetti sauce. Although Chelsea got first dibs on dinner, we still were hungry and weren't going to let this incident spoil our evening. Chuckling, we all pitched in and grabbed paper towels to clean off our section before sitting back down to enjoy what was left of Mom's meal after Chelsea's pillage.

After settling in my chair, I reached over to take a piece of warm, buttered bread from the center of the table to dip into my spaghetti. As I was chewing, I began to notice something wasn't quite right. I could feel something strange sticking to the roof of my mouth. My eyes darted down toward my plate where I realized there was dog hair in my spaghetti. Not wanting to risk further upsetting Mom by having to throw away more food, and thinking this would somehow improve Chelsea's standing with her, I swallowed all the dog hairs that were in my mouth. Disgusted, I quickly chased it with a glass of water, gulping, nearly choking—it was so refreshing. But it wasn't over yet. I was caught in a dilemma. There was still a lot of spaghetti on my plate that had dog hair in it, and at the same time, I had an angry mom sitting to my right. There was no winning with those options. Stuck between a rock and a hard place, I realized what had to be done. I paused in a prayer-like manner but didn't pray. I more so just thought in the direction of up.

Give me the strength to do this.

After sharing my thoughts with the universe, I grabbed the parmesan cheese from across the table and caked my spaghetti in it. Tightly gripping my fork, I took a deep breath, slowly released it, and plowed away at what was left on my plate. I was proud of what I had just accomplished—not folding under pressure, and doing what I thought was necessary. Ironically, after I finished my plate, I glanced over to my mom and she'd calmed down enough to laugh about the entire episode—a few dog hairs too late for me.

Wonderstruck, my mom asked, "How'd that little dog get up there?"

Moving forward, we kept a close eye on Chelsea whenever we had food on the table. But even with this heightened awareness, she still found a way to sneak past our guard from time to time and get first dibs on dinner.

There was more to Chelsea than what met the eye. She wasn't always cranky and mischievous.

I remember the first time I discovered she had a playful side under her concrete exterior; it was surprising, given she'd almost bitten me days before. One afternoon, I was folding laundry in my room and the next thing I knew, Chelsea jumped into the basket filled with the clothes. She rolled around, making herself comfortable, eventually finding herself wrapped around one of my shirts. I smiled—it was an adorable moment. Then I had a random idea to carry her around the house. I prepared the basket for her with a fleece blanket underneath for comfort. When I picked up the basket, I noticed she was staring at me in a way that I'll never forget. The innocence in her big brown eyes and the smile beaming from her face melted my heart—a moment I'll cherish forever.

Carrying Chelsea in the basket allowed her to view the world from a different perspective other than from the ground. I imagined she also loved the softness of the fleece against her fur. No matter how much I wanted to capture this moment and never let it go, eventually my scrawny arms gave out and I had to set the basket down. Even afterwards, Chelsea remained in the basket, savoring the moment—being fully present, free from wounds of the past and the worries of the future.

On April 24, 1854, Henry David Thoreau wrote in his journal, "find your eternity in every moment." Despite her traumatic past, somehow, that old dog learned to do this well—even if that moment was inside of a laundry basket.

This was her favorite game to play; it never got old. The more we did it, the stronger I seemed to get, and I could carry Chelsea in the basket just a little longer each time. Those moments we shared during this game brought us close and made me realize she wasn't that burdensome dog I had mistaken her for on day one. She just wanted to belong, and after a while, she did. It was difficult to imagine life before Chelsea.

Before I knew it, Chelsea had become part of the family—but even then, she still needed her alone time. Most days, you could find her resting on her yellow fleece dog bed downstairs by the fireplace. Her body fit in it perfectly, as if it were made just for her.

When Chelsea wasn't lounging in her comfy dog bed, she loved going out for walks. I'd put on her red leash and we'd stroll the neighborhood, pausing several times along the way as she sniffed the ground to take in all of nature's scents—the grass, the flowers, and the lingering trail of other animals. Every now and then, she'd sneak a quick pee or poo on a neighbor's lawn, and I'd stand as her lookout, ready to run with her at a moment's notice if we were busted.

Chelsea was ten years old when she first arrived at our home that summer of 2000. That's seventy in dog years, and I tried to treat her as such. I never considered myself to be her "owner," but rather a friend. I don't think animals are ever "ours." Pets come into our lives for a short time—a mere glimpse, when looking back. They give us a kind of love we never realized was needed, and then they're gone, almost as quickly as they arrived. If I've learned anything over the years, it's that time catches up to us all.

Transitioning into high school that summer, I desperately tried to press the fast-forward button on life. I naïvely believed I was ready to arrive into the future—even though the future wasn't ready for me. I was so eager to grow up, to drink my first beer, to smoke my first cigarette, to sneak out of the house, to have my first kiss. I really thought those experiences were something special, but looking back, none of those "milestones" compared to the beautiful moments I shared with Chelsea. I'd trade that first terrible cigarette for another walk with her in a heartbeat.

It only took a few weeks for Chelsea to find her way into my heart—and for me to find my way into hers. With each passing day, she was willing to be more vulnerable as I continued to meet her where she was. Trust was built as I patiently learned about her boundaries and respected them. Although Chelsea needed me that summer, I also needed her. Through that little dog, I understood the value of looking beyond the exterior of others—that if we dare explore beneath the surface, we may stumble upon something truly lovely. But more than that, what I'm most proud of is what Chelsea learned: that no matter what her past held, a new chapter of her story was being written—one where she captivated the heart of a young boy who would love her forever.

Chapter 5
Bubble Gum and Soda

After surviving eighth grade, in 2001, I became a freshman at the newest high school in our county. Life was different in those days—both for the better and worse. In a time before the emergence of smartphones, I believe people were more present, connected, and had deeper, more meaningful relationships. It's easy to reminisce about an era without the distractions of modern technology, but those days also held their fair share of hardships that I would never want to revisit.

The world was a tough place to exist for a high school freshman. While trying to fit in and dealing with zits seemed overwhelming enough, being a victim of bullying only exacerbated those enormous stresses. Back then, I think the closest thing we had to a "Stomp Out Bullying" campaign was McGruff the Crime Dog—and nobody cared for those presentations. Bullying was a part of life for an adolescent, and it was largely accepted. Dare I say it was systemic, in the sense that inaction from authority figures perpetuated its existence.

For me, the primary source of my bullying came from overt racism that wouldn't be tolerated today. I was called a "chink" for my mixed ethnicity and pushed into lockers by kids much bigger than me. In one instance, a teacher saw this very thing happen but did nothing—just stood there, a bystander. I figured if a teacher wouldn't help me, what else could I do? I was fearful of confrontation and defenseless against those older guys. And I did my best to follow advice, avoiding the routes that I knew they traveled. But it wasn't enough. Bullying didn't just happen inside of the school building; it followed me home on the bus.

During one particularly dreaded bus ride home (a memory that's haunted me for years), my head was slammed against a window as I was spat on and teased for being half Asian. I trembled in fear, being outnumbered, overpowered, and defenseless, waiting for the terror to end. The worst part was that nobody tried to defend me with either words or physical intervention. That day I understood the meaning of loneliness. I couldn't comprehend why being Asian was so wrong in their eyes. This moment destroyed my confidence and made me ashamed of being me. For a while, I was angry at God for not making me "white" enough.

Although what I went through was horrible, another kid named Billy had it worse. Billy was openly gay in a time when that was heavily taboo in the middle-class suburbs of south Atlanta. I couldn't imagine his suffering through those years. Billy was a kind soul who others preyed upon solely because of their bigotry.

It was no secret that Billy was being bullied. His mother frequented the school, bringing awareness to the administrators of what was happening to him.

One morning, I was sent to the office to run an errand for a teacher. As I was standing there, waiting my turn in line, the door slammed open with so much force that it bounced off of the rubber doorstop, hitting the person who opened it. I quickly recognized it was Billy's mother.

She stormed into the office alongside him, with righteous indignation that any mother would have, shouting, "Are you actually gonna do anything about this? You told me this would never happen again. Or are you gonna give me some more of your bullshit?"

All the hustle and bustle of the office came to an abrupt stop as everyone turned their attention toward her. I knew exactly what incident she was talking about.

Every day, before homeroom, the students who arrived earlier would hang out in the cafeteria. This time was a social hub filled with cliques, where you were only as important as the people you were seen sitting beside. In all of its shallowness, it was the peak of our day—a time to show off your new shoes, a time to check out that girl or guy you were interested in, and a time to become someone important.

Billy was sitting alone in the back of the cafeteria when I saw a familiar gang of troublemakers, known for their disdain toward authority and antics that often resulted in suspension, approach and sit with him. Jeff, their ringleader, exchanged words with Billy, but from my distant seat I couldn't hear what was being said. To my surprise, Billy was smiling, and I couldn't figure out why. At first sight, it looked as if those guys were befriending him. But that made little sense—it didn't align with their toxic reputations. As Jeff was talking to Billy, Shawn, one of Jeff's goons, discreetly stood up, walked around the table, gave a quick glance to the others, and snickered as he touched Billy's back in a seemingly friendly manner. Although something about this scenario didn't sit right with me, I didn't spend much more time thinking about it.

Billy and I shared homeroom together, and that morning I arrived early. Only a few people were in the classroom, including the teacher. I found my desk, took out a notebook, and chatted up a friend awaiting the bell. Everything seemed to be business as usual.

A few minutes passed before Billy arrived, wearing his typical upbeat smile that exuded positive vibes wherever he went. As he was setting his backpack down, pink goo-like strands stretched between the backpack and his back, connecting them together in a sticky mess—it was chewed gum. This was the scheme that Jeff and his gang were up to that morning under the guise of friendship. Billy stood in disbelief, trying to hold the tears back. His spirit was broken, violated by those who pretended to be his friend. Some people laughed when he could no longer keep his composure, shaking as tears ran down his face before fleeing the classroom, completely humiliated.

I empathized with his suffering and couldn't help but feel sorry for him.

Later that day, I ran into Jeff and Shawn in the restroom. I was at the urinal when I heard them trudging in like a pack of hyenas. They were snickering.

"What a fag! I heard he cried like a little bitch and had to go home."

Those words enraged me as adrenaline pumped through my veins, fueling a call to justice for Billy. But at the same time, I was afraid of what they may do to me if I were to speak up. Routed by my fears, I remained silent as I zipped up my pants and walked over to the sink to wash my hands. They continued their conversation, poking fun at Billy as I listened, disgusted both by their cruelty and my inability to call them out on it. I pressed down on the handle of the paper towel dispenser, grabbing just enough to dry my hands, and exited. While I may have left the restroom physically unscathed, my character was not—I was a coward.

This incident revealed to me who I was and who I obviously was not. When I was a kid, I wanted to be like Russell Crowe's character, Maximus, in Gladiator. I envied his courage, especially in this moment of self-preservation. It was soul-crushing to know I was far from being that hero I desperately yearned to be.

When I arrived home that afternoon, I immediately went upstairs to my room. I shut the door, making sure it was locked, and cried, weighed down by the utter disgrace of my cowardliness. Time passed slowly as I laid there, swollen eyes red and congested before hearing the familiar clanking of Chelsea's dog tags. She clawed at the door as I did my best to ignore her, wallowing in self-pity. Chelsea eventually stopped but made it clear she wanted to come into the room as I noticed her little paws barely poking through the gap between the bottom of the door and the carpet.

Admiring her persistence, I finally gave in, unlocking the door and opening it as she burst inside with an unusual upbeat energy. She jumped all over my legs in pure excitement—her way of asking me to pick her up. I obliged and carried her over to the bed where we laid down together. As she nuzzled up closely against my chest, she licked the tears off of my face, comforting me through my pain. Chelsea's presence was the soft landing I needed, reassuring me I was being a little hard on myself, and courageous or not, I was still loved.

This moment brought me hope that all was not lost—and maybe one day I'd have enough courage to stand up for what was right and become a hero. Ralph Waldo Emerson reminds us, "Our chief want is someone who will inspire us to be what we know we could be." Chelsea is that someone who did that for me.

A few weeks later, an opportunity to redeem myself would unexpectedly arrive. It was just another day at school, squeezing through the overcrowded hallways, going from one class to another, when I noticed Shawn was right in front of me, totally vulnerable. I knew this was my chance to do something that would render justice for what he'd done to Billy. Anger surged up in me as I remembered that day and how I felt when they made

fun of him in the restroom. My heart raced as
a thousand thoughts rushed through my brain,
contemplating my next move.

The window to take action was dwindling as I found
myself caught in a conundrum. Initially, I just wanted
to sucker punch this guy. But after more deliberation, I
realized I didn't want to get into trouble; I just wanted
him to have a taste of his own medicine.

Then the idea struck me like an epiphany from the
heavens. I could even hear the imaginary orchestra
playing music in my head, validating that this was the
right path to follow. I decided to stick gum on Shawn's
back, like he'd done to Billy.

There was a pack of gum in my pocket, which I
quickly opened up and chewed vigorously, five sticks
at once, letting it absorb all my saliva. Removing it
from my mouth, I wadded the chewed gum into a ball.
Though I was ready to strike, I proceeded cautiously
knowing I couldn't lift his backpack and stick gum on
him without him noticing. This challenge caused me to
second-guess myself to the point of nearly giving up on
the plan.

But then, for whatever reason, Chelsea flashed into
mind, along with the beautiful moment we'd shared in
my room days before, inspiring me to be what I knew
I could be—courageous. Now whether sticking gum
on Shawn's back was a virtuous application of courage,
that's an argument for another day. Regardless, because
of that little dog, I certainly felt courageous and chose
to move forward.

Navigating the congested halls, I slowly unzipped his backpack and stretched the gum out all over the top of his books, then zipped it up without him noticing. Those around me were stunned, gasping at my boldness for doing this to Shawn, a six-foot-three bully, who would've easily kicked my ass. To my surprise, there wasn't as much satisfaction in doing this as I imagined; I believed I'd feel heroic. But honestly, I just felt empty and insignificant. It turned out to not be the climactic and valiant moment I was seeking after all. Instead of accepting that reality and moving on, I interpreted this lack of fulfillment as simply meaning I didn't do enough to ensure justice was carried out for Billy. That being my only explanation, I concluded that I needed to do something else—something more drastic. I couldn't let this hang in the balance, but I was running out of time. I had to act now.

Realizing it was a now or never situation, without much thought, I did something that I'm sure those bystanders will always remember. There was a soda in my bag that I planned on drinking in class, but in a stroke of genius, I decided to put it to better use. Throwing caution to the wind, I opened Shawn's backpack once again, undetected, and poured the entire bottle of soda into his bag.

Those around me who witnessed this were even more shocked than they were about the gum. Their eyes widened and jaws dropped, at a total loss for words, trying to process what I had just done. Adrenaline kept me focused and unfazed as I zipped up Shawn's backpack in the nick of time, right before the bell rang.

Shawn and I didn't have any classes together, and I never found out how he reacted. To my surprise (and ultimately, my well-being), he never discovered it was me—until now, that is, if he's reading this book.

But most importantly, to my knowledge, he never messed with Billy again. The bubble gum and soda had certainly done their job.

I doubt God is smiling at me for what happened that day, but I was only doing what I thought was best. However, maybe it was, in part, out of a selfish ambition to reclaim the piece of myself I'd lost the day I remained silent, consumed by fear in that bathroom.

Either way, when I recall that moment in my room with Chelsea, I can't help but remember how she made me feel loved when I felt unlovable. She couldn't have cared less whether or not I was courageous; to her, I was enough, and she loved me regardless of my shortcomings. Victor Hugo articulates this truth so precisely in his novel, *Les Misérables*: "The supreme happiness of life is the conviction that we are loved; loved for ourselves, or rather in spite of ourselves."

Without Chelsea's support, I wouldn't have stood up to that bully. And more than that, I may never have seen myself as someone who could ever demonstrate courage, given my failed track record of it. But thanks to her, I found my true self again.

Chapter 6

"Her Name's Lexi."

Before I knew it, seasons changed, and the years went by as quickly as days. I found myself maturing (somewhat), though not so much that you'd think I was responsible.

My senior year of high school had snuck up on me, and I was excited to experience everything seniors look forward to—prom, graduation, and turning eighteen, a milestone into adulthood. But at the same time, it was difficult watching Chelsea age.

The first noticeable difference was in her mobility. She had trouble climbing the stairs while also not preferring to be carried up or down them. She'd often enjoy basking in the sun's rays that beamed through the windows as she slept the days away in her comfy yellow bed. Her accidents in the house became more frequent, reminding me that time doesn't discriminate against any of us. It was heartbreaking. This senior rescue dog had spent most of her life absent of love, and the timer was counting down on the most joyful chapter of her life. Time was going faster than I wanted to admit—it seemed unfair.

Chelsea was with me through some of the most pivotal years of my life. She watched me grow up during the last year of middle school and throughout all of high school. But now it was 2004, and she was fourteen years old—the bottom tier of her breed's average lifespan. While her life seemed to be coming to an end, mine was just getting started. I couldn't wait for high school to be over. Now that it had arrived, part of me wished I could've turned back time. I never considered what those four years would do to my canine companion.

I fought hard to push away the fact that she didn't have much time left. Even when I felt successful in doing so, the dreadful thought always lingered in the back of my mind.

One afternoon, I was upstairs watching TV when I heard the creaky garage door swing open and quickly shut. Not caring who was arriving home, I continued enjoying my show until a familiar shout interrupted my leisure time.

"Kerk, come downstairs!"

It was my mom. This is what she normally did when she needed something from me, rarely ever coming up the stairs to get my attention. I could never tell if I was in trouble or not. Whether she was calling me downstairs to grab my laundry or to scold me about something, her tone never changed.

Unable to think of any reason I should've been in trouble, I figured she just wanted me to grab my laundry from the dryer. Being in no rush, I took my time, sitting there a while longer, enjoying the rest of the show and delaying the inevitable. I hated folding clothes (and still do to this day).

I heard her voice call again, "Kerk, where are you?"

Like a typical teenager, I didn't reply and grudgingly trudged down the stairs, cussing at her in my mind.

Damn, this better be some urgent shit. We ain't got no DVR, and she's making me miss my show.

I arrived in the living room, making it apparent by my tone that I was irritated.

"Mom, what do you... "

Before I could finish my question, I stopped in disbelief, observing that my mom wasn't alone. She smiled and spoke up, providing some clarity to the situation. "Her name's Lexi."

Lexi was a border collie and lab mix who was born on the fourth of July in 2004—the newest addition to our family. She was gifted to my mom from Deborah, a friend and favorite client.

Unable to contain my excitement, I rushed over toward Lexi and embraced her. As I knelt down at her level, she jumped all over me, scratching my chest and neck in her attempt to lick my face. I brushed my hands through Lexi's beautiful black coat, noticing her tiny tail wag back and forth as we continued to play. Her ears perked up as she rolled over onto her back, pulling her paws in toward herself, mimicking the arms of a T-Rex. I laughed and gave her a belly rub, which only made this high energy pup more rambunctious.

I was immediately enamored with Lexi, but Chelsea certainly was not.

The new-puppy energy Lexi brought to the house was a bit much for Chelsea. In her old age, Chelsea enjoyed keeping to herself—and as you can imagine, Lexi, being a puppy, was the complete opposite. Any time Chelsea attempted to enjoy her afternoon naps in solitude, Lexi could be found nearby, constantly demanding her to play.

In the beginning, Lexi was much smaller than Chelsea. In fact, she was so tiny that her whole body could fit onto one of my shoulders—where she often sat, licking my ear and gnawing at my hair. It was truly precious.

But within a couple of months, Lexi grew to be much bigger than Chelsea—though she didn't seem to be aware of this fact. Lexi would roughhouse with Chelsea to the point that her play was mistaken for aggression. Chelsea would snap back, thinking she was defending herself, while Lexi stood perplexed by her sudden hostility. It didn't take long before Lexi learned to leave Chelsea alone, after nearly getting nipped on more than a few instances.

Training the new pup seemed to be a breeze—mostly because I wasn't the one who had to do it. This was Mom's role, falling on her by default since she'd brought her home; at least that's the excuse I told myself to avoid extra responsibility. Regardless, I was impressed at the progress Lexi was making, both in potty training and general obedience. My mom did a wonderful job.

Although Mom was her primary caretaker, we all had to play our part in making sure she didn't have any accidents in the house. We rotated shifts, reinforcing

outdoor potty training. Lexi was a brilliant listener
and always responded when being called. Despite not
having a fenced-in backyard, we could let her roam free,
leash-less, without a worry in the world.

Watching Lexi embrace her youth was refreshing.
Whenever we let her outside, she'd zoom around as if
it were her first time feeling grass beneath her paws.
She'd create a trail of wind as she blazed back and
forth between the maple tree and the honeysuckle
bush—which was enough to push back her ears and
lips, revealing a smile. The way she'd prance through
the yard, as if she were a deer, was so elegant—it was
truly a majestic sight, and invigorating to the soul.

I'll never forget when I first discovered Lexi had
learned how to manage her high energy around an aging
Chelsea. During the wee hours of Christmas break
2004, I was dead tired, having binge-played video games
for the last nine hours. This was a treat that wouldn't
happen on school nights. I stumbled downstairs with
heavy eyes to grab water before heading to bed. As I
arrived at the bottom of the stairs and stepped into
the living room, what I saw immediately stopped me
in my tracks. Suddenly I became alert, rubbing my
eyes, not sure if I was dreaming. Lexi and Chelsea
were actually playing together. This was astonishing,
as months before this would've never happened. But
something had clearly changed since then—there was
growth. Lexi was being so gentle with her, respecting
her boundaries, and not pushing too hard.

It was wonderful watching two animals from opposite life paths coming together to share this beautiful moment of mutual vulnerability—setting aside the past to move toward a better future. I smiled, pausing in awe, enjoying this milestone in their relationship, but only watching a moment longer before my eyes became too heavy and I had to sleep.

Over the next few months, Chelsea and Lexi became inseparable, playing regularly and even taking naps together. Sharing that season of life with them and witnessing their love grow for one another was nothing short of captivating.

In his book, *Blue Light*, Walter Mosley writes, "We are not trapped or locked up in these bones. No, no. We are free to change. And love changes us. And if we can love one another, we can break open the sky."

Looking back, this is what Lexi and Chelsea taught me through their relationship—that love does change us. They both had lived incredibly different lives and were trying to figure out how to coexist in the same environment. Lexi lived in an ideal world, never knowing a day without love. Chelsea was her counterpart, blemished with scars, living most of her life absent of love. While their first chapter together wasn't pleasant, these two dogs took what love they had, shared it with one another, and wrote a new ending for themselves. I was overwhelmed with gratitude to witness this happen, especially knowing that Chelsea didn't have much time left. Being present as their love blossomed brought me immense joy, so much so that seventeen years later, I still reminisce about that winter—I miss both of them tremendously.

Crystal with Spartacus and Maximus on their birthday.

Chelsea lounging in her comfy dog bed.

Taking Chelsea out for a walk in 8th grade.

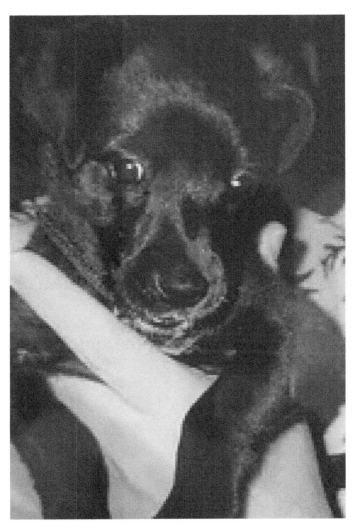

"Her name's Lexi."

Part 2
The Storm

"When you come out of the storm,
you won't be the same person who walked in."

—Haruki Murakami

Chapter 7
Two Scared Kids

During the spring of 2005, the last semester of my senior year in high school, I couldn't have been happier with life. I had two magnificent dogs, an Xbox, and a girlfriend I had been dating for a few months. We'll call her "Emma." Back then it felt like love, but in hindsight, I was naïve and more in love with the idea of being with her.

One day, while I was sitting on the couch and playing video games, I heard her calling my name as she walked up the stairs of my parents' house. I was barely paying attention, but she was visible in my peripheral vision.

"Kerk, we need to talk... it's important... Please."

I was too consumed with Bungie Studio's recent release of Halo 2 to recognize the urgency in her voice. Heck, I wouldn't have even noticed if the house was on fire. This pinnacle masterpiece was a milestone in gaming history and was truly remarkable for its time. To fully comprehend my love for this game, I actually declined a family vacation to Hawaii in order to stay home and play it with my friend David. I suppose you could say I was addicted, but I'd like to think that I was just fully committed to my growth as a gamer.

"Chill out, Emma. Let me just arm this bomb; we're about to win the match."

She didn't understand. We were playing a rival clan on Lockout, which was my favorite map. And now suddenly she wanted to talk? How dare she?

"God freaking' dang it! We just lost—look what you made me do! I freakin' died because of you."

I furiously threw my headset onto the ground along with the controller. "We were so freakin' close. God!"

The controller hit the floor so hard that it bounced like a tennis ball, skipping across the carpet.

It felt like minutes went by as an awkward silence filled the room after my post-defeat tantrum. But in reality, only seconds had passed before I calmed down enough to address her in my attempt to ease the tension.

"Okay, now what was so important?"

I hadn't noticed her smeared makeup from the streams of tears running down her face. I'd never seen her like this—so distraught and disheveled.

I had met Emma just six months earlier on MySpace, the top social media platform of the day. On MySpace, you could arrange your friends in tiers of importance known as your "Top 4"—an unnecessary feature that I'm convinced was the source of many ruined friendships.

Emma was always so well put together and a free spirit—she was beautiful. But here she stood, a complete wreck. This was uncharted territory for us in the short duration of our relationship.

"Emma, what... what in the world happened?"

I paused and waited for what seemed to be an eternity. Trembling and crying uncontrollably, she could barely get her words out.

"Kerk... I... I'm... "

Before she could finish, my heart began pounding so loudly that I could clearly hear its individual beats, feeling like it was going to explode out of my chest. I was expecting the worst as fear overwhelmed me, dreading Emma's next words. Somehow, I knew what she was about to say. I'm not exactly sure what gave it away, but I suspect it was the pent-up anxiety from our foolish teenage indiscretions, compounded with the constant stress of wondering if it would ever catch up to us.

Emma gathered herself enough to murmur the words that would break any seventeen-year-old guy:

"I'm pregnant."

Her crying eerily halted so promptly that it seemed as if she'd just hit the "off" switch. Looking back, I think she had cried so much there wasn't a single tear left in her small frame.

I sat there speechless and in total shock. The first thing I thought about was how my parents were going to react, mostly contemplating how disappointed they would be in me. I couldn't help but wonder if they'd actually follow through and kick me out of the house, as they had "playfully" threatened if I were to ever get a girl pregnant. I hadn't been in much trouble in my life until this point. The fear of disappointing them kept me on the straight and narrow. I loved making them happy and felt most loved when they were happy with me.

Growing up, my parents did everything they could to ensure my life was better than what they had experienced as children. From their abusive and empty childhoods grew a commitment to setting up their children with the greatest opportunities to be successful in life—the same opportunities that were unjustly stolen from them. I felt sorry for my parents. As children, life had short-changed them, but somehow they turned out to be wonderful. I could only imagine where they would be if life had dealt them the same cards it had dealt to me.

In their attempts to help me succeed, my parents drove me to excel in school and sports, which they believed would give me a leg up in life somewhere down the road. Unbeknownst to them, I interpreted these well-placed intentions as meaning that my worthiness of being loved was contingent on my grades in school and performance on the field. It was great when I made all As, scored a touchdown, or won that wrestling match. But on the other side of that coin, I carried the crushing shame of being unlovable whenever I fell short of those daunting standards.

At times, I felt like I was barely keeping my head above water, struggling to swim against the raging current toward the finish line of perfection. It was emotionally and physically draining to constantly seek their approval through performance-based love, an unsustainable expectation. The idea I could achieve my worthiness seemed so normal to me, I thought everyone else was striving for the same thing. This impossible aspiration was the source of my childhood wound, which became my identity for several years—that I was never enough.

Emma remained standing, quietly waiting for my response. The room was so silent you could've heard a pin drop on the floor. I sat there a few minutes longer, lost for words and unsure of what to do. When my heart rate slowed down enough to resume beating a normal rhythm, the news that I was going to be a teenage father truly sank in. Before I could speak, Emma broke her silence.

"What are we gonna do, Kerk?"

After mentally walking through the fact that our lives would never be the same again, I said the only thing that came to mind: "I don't know."

The blank stare on Emma's face told me that my uncertainty wasn't helping the situation. She was looking to me for reassurance, but hell, I was in the same boat as she was, lost upstream without a paddle. Seeking comfort, she walked over to the couch, sat down next to me, grabbed my hand, and laid her head on my shoulder.

The fear of the unknown was unbearable. Our dreams of a bright future were gone, just like that. We were two scared kids holding onto one another, hoping this would somehow make it all go away. For the first time in our relationship, we both were broken and sobbed together on that couch.

Later that night, after Emma had left, I felt a loneliness that made me sick to my stomach. Not knowing what was to become of our lives overwhelmed me—a load too heavy for any seventeen-year-old to carry. I didn't know who to tell or who I could trust to keep it a secret. I couldn't tell my parents—I wasn't quite ready to be disowned. And if I got kicked out of the house, I'd have to work several jobs to support Emma, myself, and our child, which would leave no time to play Halo 2. Yes, that was actually a concern of mine. By now, you shouldn't be surprised.

My brother and sister were too young to understand. They might tattle, not out of malice, but it's what brothers and sisters do. They enjoy getting the other in trouble with the parents—it's just part of the deal. But, this was sensitive information that obviously required the security clearance above that of bloodlines.

I didn't need anyone to lecture me on my mistakes—the sins of my past were here to remind me of that. I needed someone to be there and just to sit with me. I wanted it to be Chelsea, but because of her physical limitations, she needed to stay downstairs. I felt bad about disturbing her while she rested. With what time she had left to enjoy life, I didn't want her spending her remaining days being drowned in my problems—although I'm sure she would've loved being there for me.

Completely exhausted from the emotional toll of the day's events, I couldn't wait to go to sleep.

After getting ready for bed that night, I headed back upstairs to my room, finding Lexi laying on my bed as if it were her own. This wasn't something she normally did, but tonight I needed company more than ever. My mom didn't really like Lexi on the beds or couches because of the hair she'd leave behind. But that night, I didn't care. I shut the door, turned out the lights, and cuddled up next to her.

Doris Day is credited with saying, "I have found that when you are deeply troubled, there are things you get from the silent devoted companionship of a dog that you can get from no other source."

Lexi's presence was that for me; so calming I was able to lose myself in the moment, nearly forgetting about my troubles from earlier that day. Eventually I told her everything that had happened, but she didn't seem fazed. In her mind, nothing had changed. I shared with her all of my fears and worries, talking her ears off until I arrived at that in-between place of being awake and asleep. But before I completely dozed off, my last thoughts were peaceful. Being reassured through Lexi's unwavering companionship, I was able to let go and let tomorrow take care of itself.

Chapter 8
A Breath of Fresh Air

The next morning, I woke up earlier than usual but not on purpose. I was roused from my sleep by what sounded like monsoon rains beating down on the roof. There was barely any light coming through the window as I stretched out my arms and legs across the bed before sitting up. I wasn't yet fully awake, hoping the day before had only been a bad dream. But to my dismay, it hadn't. I noticed Lexi was already up and waiting by the bedroom door to be let out.

Opening the bedroom door, I was caught completely off guard when I saw Emma on the living room couch, drenched from the storm. I knew the rest of my family was still sleeping and couldn't have let her in. They would've woken me, letting me know I had company. Then it dawned on me that she probably used the spare key under the plant on the porch to let herself in. I previously told her she could use it anytime, as she had in the past to set up random surprises for me. But before I could ask any questions, she quickly paced toward me with intention. Her demeanor was unlike yesterday. There were no tears running down her cheeks, and the focus in her eyes told me she meant business.

She grasped my hand. "Kerk, we can't have this baby. I'll look like a slut, and our parents will disown us. We can't do this."

Despite any truth in what she had just said, I tried reassuring her, "We can do this. I won't go to college. I'll get two jobs. I'll do whatever it takes for us. It's that simple."

It was at this moment that those familiar tears from yesterday showed up on her face once again. "No, Kerk... we just can't."

Saying nothing else, she loosened her grip on my hand and kissed me on the cheek before walking out of the house and driving away. I'm not sure where she went, but I didn't hear from her for the rest of the week.

Emma's words were music to my ears. The weight of the world had lifted off of my shoulders so instantaneously that Atlas would've envied me. Deep down, I was relieved she felt this way. The thought of us being teenage parents was overwhelming at best. Heck, it was hard enough making sure all of my dirty clothes ended up in the laundry basket (and not next to it).

Life looked hopeful as the universe granted me a second chance at a "normal" life instead of one as a teenage parent. My shallow dream of becoming a plastic surgeon, driving my Ferrari down Rodeo Drive, and partying with supermodels felt possible again. Thankfully for everyone's sake, not a single part of that dream came true. Can you actually imagine me operating on you?

Although Emma never clarified what she meant by not having the baby, I knew exactly what she was implying. We never once used the "A" word—you know, abortion. It was such a taboo word and was easier on our consciences to neither say it nor address it for what it really was—the intentional destruction of life. Even worse, it was the life of our future child.

Just a year earlier, I became a Christian during an emotionally charged chapel service at the private school I attended. There were two main issues that I remember were always at the center of debate at that school: gay marriage and abortion.

I remember a heated exchange when Hillary, a pious and outspoken classmate, raised her voice while pointing her finger at someone else. "Abortion is murder. And homosexuals are going to Hell. It's a fact!"

As a new Christian, I didn't know what to think. I just sat there, observing and soaking it all in. I don't think Hillary had bad intentions, but she could've at least worked on her delivery a little.

In my current situation, her words echoed throughout my mind. The more I thought about what Hillary said, the worse I felt about this whole thing.

Was abortion really murder?

The next week, after not hearing a word from Emma, not even a text, I reached out to check on her.

During our conversation, I couldn't help but bring up the question that was lingering in my mind.

"Do you think we're murderers, Emma?"

She responded defensively, as if I were accusing her, "I don't know, Kerk, but I'd rather not talk about it. I need to go."

She hung up before I could reply. Our communication over the next few weeks was just as brief as that conversation. It was disheartening that the one person who understood the emotional complexity of the entire situation would barely speak to me.

Finally, she texted me the morning of the abortion: "We're going to Atlanta later. I've booked the procedure. Pick you up soon."

We said little on the drive there—small talk about songs on the radio—attempting to break the awkward silence. Although I've tried to forget that car ride to the abortion clinic, I'll never forget what I witnessed inside of that cold and eerie waiting room—a memory that still haunts me.

Upon arrival to the clinic, I immediately knew I had no business being there. The rundown facility with its outdated decor, moldy ceilings, and torn carpets was just as sketchy as I had imagined. As Emma was filling out some paperwork at the front desk, I saw a girl who couldn't have been over sixteen years old sitting with an older man, who I assumed was her father. She was visibly distressed, scared out of her mind, trembling and crying. She looked over at him, pleading.

"I don't wanna do it. Please don't make me do it. I'll do anything."

It was heart-wrenching to watch another human being display so much anguish and vulnerability in a room full of strangers.

Her father looked at her with disgust and, without shame, belittled her in front of everyone, sticking his finger right in her face. "Quit making a scene. Are you tryin' to piss away your future? You're gonna do it. So shut your damn mouth. If you weren't such a whore, we wouldn't be here."

After that man trampled on what dignity she had left, I looked around and saw that no one, aside from me, seemed fazed by what he'd just said to her—I didn't speak up, though I should've. No one deserves that kind of treatment. I've always wondered what happened to that girl and hope she's okay.

Emma was called to the back room shortly after that episode. I sat there alone in the lobby, trying to distract myself by playing "Snake" on my Nokia phone. I couldn't wait to get out of that dark place.

I was so immersed in playing the game that I didn't even notice Emma standing in front of me after she was finished.

She tapped me on the shoulder. "Kerk, let's go."

The car ride home was just as silent as the one up there. When we arrived at my house, she dropped me off and could barely look at me. Maybe she felt ashamed. I'll never know. But I wasn't mad at her for being distant—we all carry trauma differently.

It was late and everyone was already sleeping, including Lexi, when I walked through the front door. That night,

I went to bed with a guilty conscience, realizing that I couldn't undo what had just happened. Weeks before, I thought I'd be celebrating this moment as a second chance from the universe, but I couldn't have been more wrong. I felt so alone.

A thousand questions flooded my mind, along with racing emotions I could barely process. One thought came to mind that stood out:

Who would my child have been?

In his novel, *Message in a Bottle*, Nicholas Sparks writes, "I feel an emptiness in my soul. I find myself searching the crowds for your face—I know it's an impossibility, but I cannot help myself."

Even to this day, there are moments that I still wonder about that question; but I try not to dwell on it, afraid I'll end up in a dark place that I can't crawl out of.

As I lay there in my bed, sobbing for the loss of my child, it surprised me to hear a familiar scratching at the door—Lexi. I immediately rolled over, throwing the covers off of me, and got up to let her in. She jumped all over me in excitement, just like the moment we met. Looking into Lexi's eyes, it was hard not to smile. I shut the door behind her as she leaped onto the bed, bouncing around playfully. I was too tired to play, but I couldn't resist her charm. Wagging her tail, Lexi rolled over on her back—her way of asking for a belly rub. And without hesitation, I complied. We played for almost an hour, wearing both of us out, which led to a good night's rest.

Lexi's presence was the breath of fresh air I needed, reminding me that life certainly goes on and that no matter what I've done, I'm still loved.

Because of the dangerous procedure, Emma ended up becoming extremely ill, needing bed rest for nearly a week. I made every effort to take care of her, offering to bring her soup and run any random errands. She declined my help.

The abortion took its toll on our relationship, and things were never the same after that day. Slowly, we grew apart, eventually breaking up a few months later. We haven't spoken since. It's been seventeen years since that life-altering day at the clinic. I truly pray that Emma has found peace and closure.

At seventeen, I naïvely thought any consequences from the abortion would resolve quickly, without the years of therapy and medication that followed. Back then, I never believed this abortion would cause so much agony—yet it did. Over the next year, it became the source of darkness that dwelled in my soul, nearly costing me everything.

Chapter 9
Lantern in The Darkness

It was the summer of 2005, and I had never felt so far away from God or from myself. High school graduation, a milestone for many, felt meaningless. At the graduation party my parents hosted, family and friends offered congratulations and shared how the next stage of life would be amazing. I wondered if they would've felt the same if they'd known my secret.

Only a few months had passed since the abortion, still fresh in my mind, and I was ashamed to allow others into my darkness. It was a silent tragedy slowly consuming my soul. Hillary's words often revisited me, "Abortion is murder." I wrestled with this statement, uncertain if it was true. But something in me must have believed it, at least partially.

I didn't feel like myself, although life went on. That summer, I often hid my feelings behind other activities to keep my mind preoccupied. I spent most of my time playing video games. In one instance, I played *Halo 2* for twenty-eight consecutive hours, only getting up to use the bathroom or stuff my face with pizza. When I wasn't gaming or sleeping, I was at the gym. Sometimes I would go twice a day, even as late as two in the morning, blasting music on my MP3 player, hoping to drown out the noise screaming in my head.

Murderer!

Even though I physically got into great shape that summer, I was far from being mentally healthy. I had so many unanswered questions that constantly tormented me.

What would people think if they found out?
Am I going to Hell?
Will God ever love me again?

With each passing day, I hated myself more. I envied everyone else's life, imagining they had it together. The stories we tell ourselves affect our perception of the world. Influencing our thoughts, which precede beliefs, and ultimately drive our actions. The story I told myself sounded like this:

I'm a murderer, a hypocrite, and God hates me.

This toxic self view eventually triggered nightmares that still find me from time to time to this day. Almost instantaneously, I understood these were visits from the demons of my past. I'd try to fight back, but their physical strength was indescribable, often paralyzing me, where I could only speak and not move. What made it worse was that no matter what they did, I would never die, feeling every bit of pain without an end in sight. It was truly my Hell.

Eventually, I'd wake up terrified, in tears, breathless, and feeling like God hated me. These nightmares would occur four to six times per week. I was scared beyond imagination to go to sleep or even close my eyes when I washed my face. I was constantly in a state of sleep deprivation and didn't know how to get help. Figuring people would think I was crazy if I told them what was happening to me, I kept it to myself.

During that summer, I needed Lexi more than ever. The fear of sleeping ruled my life, as I didn't dare go to bed by myself. Lexi was a great support; her companionship eased my fears so I could fall asleep, knowing I wasn't alone.

Although this season of life was miserable, one of my cherished memories with Lexi would be made in this era. Several nights that summer we stayed up late watching infomercials together as we drifted off to sleep. I was a sucker for them, sometimes spending ridiculous amounts of money on novelty products that I'd never use. Sometimes I'd even do an infomercial impression for Lexi, using an over-the-top salesperson voice, just to see the adorable look on her face as she would tilt her head and raise her ears in curiosity.

"You can have all of this for only five easy payments of $49.95. But wait, if you order now, we'll knock off not just one, or two, but *three* of those payments. Your satisfaction guaranteed!"

I think I enjoyed those moments far more than she did. Regardless, they brought laughter into a room that felt so insidious, I avoid it to this day. Whenever I'd wake up from nightmares, Lexi was there at ground zero, licking away my tears, and giving me the reassurance of safety to fall back asleep. For weeks, I was terrified to enter my room day or night. Because of Lexi's companionship, I found a new confidence—she was my pillar of strength. With each passing night spent together, I noticed the nightmares were slowly subsiding, along with the fear of going to sleep. Before I knew it, the nightmares that had enslaved me for so long disappeared.

Lexi became more than just a dog to me that summer. She was my confidant, a lantern in the darkness, an angel undercover. Whenever I think of her today, I realize just how fortunate I was to have her as a friend—to have known Lexi was to have known love.

In hindsight, it's much easier to see God didn't actually hate me then, nor did He ever leave my side. In the novel *Crime and Punishment*, Fyodor Dostoevsky writes, "The darker the night, the brighter the stars. The deeper the grief, the closer is God!"

Looking back, I've come to believe during those times of suffering, God was more present than ever. He relentlessly loved me from a place I could accept, through the affections of my canine companion.

Chapter 10
The Last Walk

As the summer of 2005 flew by, I was both excited and dreading going away to college that fall. It would be my first taste of freedom, living among new friends with all the unsupervised partying and skipping class whenever I pleased. On the downside, I couldn't bring Lexi to live in the dorms. I wasn't sure how'd I fare without her—she was my everything.

Also, making things more difficult, Chelsea was aging quickly, and I knew she had little time left. It was truly a sad sight to see how time had taken its toll on my old friend. Despite my reservations about leaving, I was beyond ecstatic to experience the college life.

I'll never forget the day I moved away to college. I took Chelsea on the last walk we would share together—not knowing she would cross over the Rainbow Bridge less than a month later. After an early morning breakfast, I

pressed open our creaky screen door to let her outside.
She trotted along slowly through the front yard, leaving
a trail of her pawprints in the dew on the grass until
something caused her to suddenly halt. She paused
and looked up, staring curiously—there was a yellow
butterfly fluttering around her head. And to Chelsea's
delight, that butterfly landed on her snout.

She was captivated as she stood there, frozen in time,
lost in the moment. The warmth of the sun's rays, the
gentle breeze on her face, the scent of the morning
mist, and the new friend that she had just made were
Chelsea's joys in life.

In the devotional *Beyond Words*, Frederick Buechner
reminds us, "Here is the world. Beautiful and terrible
things will happen. Don't be afraid."

That senior rescue dog had been through God knows
what trauma during her fourteen years on Earth.
Despite her suffering at the hands of another, she
didn't allow her past to define how she would live
the remainder of her life. Chelsea didn't wait for the
much deserved apology that would never arrive before
allowing herself to move on. Instead, she chose to live
for those beautiful things that were awaiting her.

During that fall semester, those nightmares I thought
were gone revisited me. Without Lexi's presence, the
fear of sleeping became more intense than before. As a
result, my life spun out of control quicker than I could
fully grasp. The constant sleep deprivation affected my
grades and I spiraled into a deep depression, which only

magnified the shame from the abortion earlier that year. I was absolutely *miserable*.

I knew I needed help, but could not bring myself to seek it out, fearing I would be seen as weak, broken, and vulnerable to judgment.

Some of my friends reached out and checked on me whenever I missed classes, even offering their notes. In the few classes I did attend, most of the time I was under the influence. Surprisingly, I was never called out by any of my professors. Before I knew it, the once straight-laced, 3.87 GPA student everyone had known in high school was failing college. The university took away my scholarship and ended up placing me on academic probation. My parents were probably the most taken aback by this, since they had no idea what I was going through. I must have looked crazy to them.

It took hours mustering courage to break the news to my dad. Embarrassed to admit I was a disappointment and yet in need of his help, I finally called.

"I need $800 or they're gonna kick me out of school."

He hesitantly gave me the money under the condition that this would never happen again.

"Dad, I'm sorry. I promise I'll do better."

I made the promise, wanting and hoping to deliver, unsure I could do so.

Things progressively got worse as the nightmares began happening nightly. My grades weren't improving, so I dropped classes to keep from flunking out. The alcohol, drugs, and women were never enough to make me feel better. I hit rock bottom when I stole discount vodka from a liquor store one night and woke up the next day at a local diner, unable to recall how I'd gotten there.

Although I hardly remember some of those drunken outings, one evening shook me to my core. That particular night I was at a stranger's run-down apartment—completely out of it, poppin' mollies and chasing them with rum, when I received a text from my parents:

"She's gone. Chelsea died."

As I read their message, I understood this wasn't about my sister; they surely would've called about that. I knew it was Chelsea, my beloved animal companion. She'd been there for me through so much. Even though I was mostly incoherent, a lump in my throat formed and unshed tears filled my eyes. Silently, I gathered myself and left the party, not wanting anyone to see me cry. In foolish judgment, I hopped into my car and drove back to the dorms, which were about three miles away. The objects in the road and the stop lights were blurry from the drug cocktail in my system, and now tears. My reaction time was extremely slow, swerving and hitting a few construction cones on the highway. It was a miracle no one was hurt.

I'd dreaded receiving that text since leaving for college. Although I knew it was coming someday soon, that anticipation didn't help cushion the gut-wrenching pain I fell into. Stumbling back into my dorm room, reeking of alcohol and cigarette smoke, I broke down right there on the cold hard floor, crying myself to sleep.

The next morning, after talking to my parents, I found out that she more than likely died of kidney failure; this could explain her frequent accidents in the house before I left. Mom explained she let Chelsea out to use the bathroom as usual, but was gone longer than expected. When they searched for her, Chelsea was found dead by our driveway—an agonizing image to bear. I believe Chelsea knew it was her time to go, and she wanted to make herself comfortable where she enjoyed herself the most—out in nature.

I often think of my last walk with Chelsea and her capacity to be fully present—neither harboring bitterness at a painful past nor being anxious about an unknown future. For everything she didn't have in earlier years, she made the best of what was left of it by pausing to soak in all life's wondrous things.

In wishful thinking, I hope as she closed her eyes before departing this world that her yellow butterfly friend found her once again. Today, whenever I see a yellow butterfly, I'm taken back to our last walk together, along with all the beautiful moments we shared. Looking back, although we had only spent four years together, it felt like a thousand moments. Chelsea was everything my soul needed in that summer of 2000—there was no better friend a thirteen-year-old boy could've ever had. I miss her tremendously.

Chapter 11
Michael

Chelsea's death only added to the destructive path I was on from the nightmares and shame I carried from the abortion. During random visits home from college, some of my family saw this dark side of me. There was one instance when I was at a birthday party for a child of a family friend and told myself I'd stay sober, but that was short-lived. While everybody was cutting the cake, I went to the bathroom to pop some pills. Minutes later, I was so high that I literally couldn't even walk. The pills were more powerful than anything I had taken before. I had gotten them from an acquaintance so I could de-stress and deeply sleep. Falling over onto the couch in our friend's basement, I was unable to move, paralyzed from this drug. Eventually my younger sister, who was still in high school, had to carry me to her car and drive me home.

"Kerk, you're such an idiot. What's wrong with you?" She lectured me as she struggled to stuff me into the back seat of her car.

I incoherently mumbled, "I dunno, I guess everything."

Laying there in her back seat, barely conscious, I stared at the car ceiling and counted the strands of fiber hanging off of it.

When we arrived home, with all of her strength, she dragged me through the front door, up the stairs, and threw me on the bed in my room, hoping I'd just sleep it off. Hearing I was home, Lexi jumped on the bed with me in pure excitement. She quickly recognized something was wrong, as I lay unresponsive. In her effort to comfort me, she licked my face as my eyes closed and my mind slowly descended into another nightmare.

My younger sister always had her ducks in a row. I admired her; she was smart, athletic, and just a great friend. I was ashamed that she had to see me in that state—not a noble example of what it meant to be an older brother.

During another visit home, I did something I thought I'd never do in a million years. My friend David and I were planning on strutting around town, showing off in his parents' convertible. My brother, who is five years younger than me, wanted to do what any younger brother wants to do—tag along. He kept trying to get into the car after I told him he wasn't going with us. I was high at the time and irritated that he wasn't listening. In front of David and his sister, who were like a second family, I slapped my brother hard across his face, grabbed him by his shirt, and threw him on the ground like he was a rag doll. Even being under the influence, he didn't stand a chance against me. He was physically outmatched—a fact I knew.

As he stood up dusting dirt off his arms, he cried in anger and humiliation, "I'll fuckin' kill you!"

I stared at him for a second before bursting into laughter as David and I got into the car and drove away. While we were cruising down the highway, I realized just how dumb we looked riding with the top down and blaring offensive rap music. And like a ton of bricks, my conscience convicted me of what I had just done to my brother. We turned the music down, and I asked David to drop me off at my house.

I had used my physical strength to harm a completely innocent person—something heroes never do. My brother, who just wanted to be with me, was stripped of his dignity as if he were some sort of criminal. I had betrayed his trust. The shame of what I had done really sunk in as I came off of my high later that night after returning home.

That evening, I found myself alone in the house, not knowing what my family was off doing. I didn't even know where Lexi was, nor did I try to search for her because, for whatever reason, all I could think about was food. I was so hungry that I made myself five peanut butter sandwiches and scarfed them down as I sat there at the kitchen table with just my thoughts. With everything I had been going through and who I had become over the past few months, I was at the end of my rope. Somewhere along the way, I had lost myself.

After stuffing my face, I headed toward the bathroom to brush my teeth and get ready for bed. Staring in the mirror, I was completely disgusted at what I saw—a murderer, a druggie, a bully, and a complete failure. The truth was too painful to confront. And that's the moment I decided my life wasn't worth living. While I was extremely frightened by the thought, I also found peace in knowing I wouldn't have to suffer anymore.

Grabbing a towel, I wiped the excess toothpaste from my lip and walked into my parents' bedroom, shutting the door behind me. I reached into my dad's dresser, removing his pistol from the top drawer, and sat on their bed, staring down the cold metal barrel.

How did life come to this?

In those few seconds, I thought about many things, including a favorite memory with Mom. When I was five years old, we had a picnic together under the sweetgum tree in our yard, watching birds and squirrels in nature's perfect harmony. We drank tea, ate half sandwiches, and listened to music on a little yellow radio I had received for Christmas the previous year.

I also pondered my favorite memory with Dad. When I was very young, often on the weekends we'd stay up late on the couch together, eating sandwiches and chips while watching sports highlights on ESPN. After eating, he'd lay on his side, and I'd sit in the space between where his knees bent and formed a sort of triangle with the back of the couch. I fit perfectly, like I was meant to be there. I missed those days a lot.

Where'd that little boy go?

I also thought about God and how much of a disappointment I had turned out to be. I wasn't certain what was going to happen after I killed myself—if I was going to Hell or who would miss me. All I knew was that I was in too much pain to go on living.

After reminiscing about the beautiful things I experienced in life and revisiting all of my failures, I pressed the cold steel of that barrel against my face. I didn't even cry. There were no more tears left in me.

Time stood still. I placed my finger on the trigger, ready to end it all.

As I sat there with my eyes closed, I heard an unfamiliar but calming voice in my head telling me I was loved. *Could this be God?*

Still not convinced, I switched off the safety and took one last deep breath.

A strange sensation of heightened awareness overcame me. I began to hear a jingling noise coming down the hallway—it was Lexi's dog tags clanking together as she drew closer. Although the door was completely shut, somehow Lexi flung it wide open, bursting into the room, as if she were Michael the Archangel saving me from the conspiracy of evil.

She quickly assessed my demeanor and bolted toward the bed, fully aware of the severity. She ran to my rescue, licking my hand, reassuring me that things were going to be okay.

I placed the gun back in the drawer and held Lexi, thankful for her friendship. Sobbing, I realized the mistake it would've been to kill myself. I'd miss so much about living—especially the little things—a gentle breeze in the summer's heat or the colors of the leaves changing in the fall. But more importantly, I would've missed the opportunity to become the person Lexi thought I was.

In the devotional *Hunger No More*, Dillion Burroughs writes, "God is never late and rarely early. He is always exactly right on time."

Looking back, I know I wouldn't be alive without Lexi's intervention. I'm fully convinced she was no ordinary dog. On that somber night, when I almost took my life, Lexi really was Michael in disguise, my angel undercover, arriving just in time.

Chapter 12

Thanksgiving

B y the spring of 2006, life had improved significantly
for me. Through the concern of my family and
friends, I finally accepted counseling and found myself
again. The nightmares subsided, enabling me to get
more consistent sleep. My grades reflected these positive
changes, as I made nearly all A's that semester. I also
started hanging out with my roommate, Micah, and his
friends more often. He was involved with a local campus
ministry. These strangers at the Wesley House became my
new family and were a positive influence on me. At first,
it was an odd transition from hanging out with druggies
to people who were always sober. I couldn't quite fathom
how these people could live the college life surrounded by
temptation and not be drunk or high. But somehow these
weird people were doing just that. More importantly, in
spite of my perception of them, was their total acceptance

of me. The lead pastor, Bill, and his wife, Amy, were instrumental in my redemption.

Although over a decade has passed since first walking into the Wesley House, I've been able to stay in touch with Bill and Amy to this very day. They even called me recently to pray over the phone about my future. They're the kindest souls, and I hope they never change.

Because of my new tribe, I eventually stopped drinking and doing drugs. I found more joy in reigniting my relationship with God. I did, however, still feel guilty about the abortion, and although I believed God loved me, there was a voice in my head telling me I was still stained from my past. It was so easy for me to accept someone else's shortcomings and counsel them in the grace of God. But for whatever reason, I wasn't fully convinced that God had forgiven me for my past.

After college, I moved further away from my childhood home as the years went by quicker than I could count. With a career change here, and a move there, before I knew it, I was in my early thirties, married, and consumed by the demands of life. Somehow along the way, I became so busy that visiting Lexi was no longer a priority, as I was a slave to the never-ending stacks of checklists and to-dos.

Whenever I did visit, mostly on major holidays, it was always painful to see how time had aged Lexi. Thanksgiving of 2018 was extremely tough for me; I hadn't seen Lexi in almost a year, although I thought about her nearly every day. That fall I decided it was time to visit my old friend again. After a long drive across the state, I finally arrived for lunch that afternoon. As my wife and I opened the front door, we were greeted by family and friends, surrounded by the aroma of sweet potato pie. Initially, I was excited about this weekend. But when I finally saw Lexi in the corner by her bed, my heart nearly stopped. She was struggling to stand, but making every effort with her fragile body to do so—it was devastating. The whiteness of old age tinted her once dark, rich fur. Time had visibly taken its toll on the dog who had saved my life. Lexi was now fourteen, limping with bad hips, and navigating a newly blurry world with cataracts covering her eyes. She was no longer the vibrant dog I once knew at seventeen. Upon seeing her in this condition, I turned away, holding back the tears, as it reminded me of Chelsea during her last days. I paused for a moment, ignoring everything around me, only thinking about Lexi, imagining her as that puppy who sat on my shoulders, nibbling at my ears and hair. My mind drifted, remembering her as the youthful dog who had come to my rescue years before. I stopped with that thought, knowing I couldn't travel down memory lane any further if I was to keep my composure. But here was my sweet Lexi, and it was apparent she was running out of time faster than I was ready to admit.

Realizing this truth, I made sure we took several pictures that evening. Squatting down to her level, I could tell she sensed my distress, just as she always had. She leaned her head against my chest, feeling my heartbeat, reminding me things would be okay, as if I were seventeen again. I whispered in her ear as I held her for the last photo we would take together, "Lexi, I love you so much."

When the house was silent, I sobbed, realizing I had wasted years of my life chasing money. I was so angry with myself for being away far too long and regretted every career I had chosen that forced me further away from Lexi.

And for what?

Now, Lexi was dying and there wasn't any amount of money that could buy back time with my dear friend.

In the novel *All the Light We Cannot See*, Anthony Doerr writes, "Time is a slippery thing: lose hold of it once, and its string might sail out of your hands forever."

This was the first moment in my life I clearly understood that money wasn't our most valuable resource, an idol I had chased for years, separating me from my family and ultimately Lexi. Though it felt too late, I had finally realized that time is the most important asset we have in life—how I would've given anything to see Lexi vibrant and youthful again.

Over the next few days, I tried spending as much time as I could with Lexi before it was time to go back to my life, too many miles away. The remaining time we shared would never be enough, and saying goodbye wasn't any easier. My heart was broken, knowing this would probably be the last time I'd see my old friend.

How I'll always remember Chelsea.

Lexi loved jumping on my lap.

Bill and Amy from the Wesley House.

The last photo we'd take together.

Part 3
A New World

"Each friend represents a world in us,
a world possibly not born until they arrive,
and it is only by this meeting
that a new world is born."

—Anaïs Nin

Chapter 13
This Sudden Urge

Since 2013, my wife (then girlfriend) Crystal wanted us to have a dog. Despite her spamming text messages of cute animal pictures to me in an attempt to change my mind, I just wouldn't budge. To give her credit, they were pretty adorable pictures. However, we were too consumed with our careers, and I didn't want the added responsibilities that come with having a canine companion—or at least that's what I initially thought.

During autumn of 2018, my wife and I were playing video games, yet my mind wandered. Although I loved gaming *and* spending time with Crystal (of course), I couldn't focus and had this sudden urge. I'm not really sure what sparked the idea, and it was so random that it felt compulsive. I examined the thought briefly and tried to put it away. But the more I resisted it, the more difficult it became to ignore. At the point that I couldn't hold it in any longer, I took off my headset and blurted it out loud: "Let's get a dog."

Crystal paused, her doubtful eyes staring me down, as if she was trying to measure my words to determine if I was being serious or not. Not a moment later, her suspicions turned to glee. "Kerk, are you serious? Like for real, for real?" She sounded like a child on Christmas morning, who just got the go-ahead to open the presents. It was precious.

"Ya, for real, for real," I smirked.

Before I could say another word, she jumped right in. "We could even get one of those hypoallergenic dogs so we wouldn't have to clean up wads of hair throughout the house." She'd obviously done her research, awaiting this very day.

Completely elated, Crystal had spoken so quickly that I barely caught what she'd said.

"Hypoaller—what?"

"You know, those dogs that don't shed." She spoke with such confidence that it made me wonder if this was common knowledge that all humans had innately understood since the dawn of time.

"Really? That's a thing?"

Crystal looked at me strangely, confirming my query by slowly nodding her head in such a manner that let me know I'd been living under a rock my entire life.

I remained in my chair, completely awestruck at this news.

What a time to be alive, I thought to myself, reveling in the accomplishments of human ingenuity. Along with inventing blue jeans, peanut butter, and the internet, it was at this very moment that I realized humanity had officially peaked—finally creating a dog that didn't shed.

There's much debate as to whether dogs can truly be hypoallergenic. But what I can tell you is the idea that they *could* be was enough reason for me to Google search "Hypoallergenic Dogs for Sale Near Me."

Completely shocked at the search results, I convinced myself that I had mistyped the search terms or that there was some sort of error. But when I checked it again, to my dismay, there were no errors.

"What the... I don't remember dogs costing this much."

I scrolled down further, which didn't make me feel any more optimistic. I couldn't help but notice the hefty price tag, boldly and loudly jumping off the web page.

"Are they out of their freakin' minds? I could buy four Xboxes for the price they have listed for that Goldendoodle." (During this time in my life, I wasn't aware that the homeless animal population and their immense suffering was a consequence of backyard breeding. In the future, we'll be adopting from a shelter.)

Luckily, my wife was more skilled than me in searching for our future pup. It didn't take her long before she showed me a picture of a Yorkie-poo, barely three months old, with dark fur, and who was so small that he captivated our hearts at first sight. In an instant, we knew he was the one. Crystal reached out to the lady selling him. It was a done deal. We were beyond ecstatic to officially be his new dog parents. There was a slight drawback, but not one we couldn't fix. His name was Blaze. Neither of us were huge fans of that name and figured he was still young enough for us to change it without causing him any confusion.

"What should we rename him?" Crystal asked.

I paused for a moment, thinking carefully, saying names silently in my head, weighing out the options. Then it came to me. "I got it. Let's name him Maximus."

Crystal tilted her head, puzzled. "Like from *Gladiator*?"

"You already know," I said, in a matter-of-fact tone, as if the name "Maximus" could *only* be synonymous with Russell Crowe's character in the box office hit.

I patiently awaited her response, uncertain if she would go for it. Previously in our relationship, I'd deferred to her when it came to these types of decisions. For example, when it came to decorating our house, she'd selected all the colors for the cabinets, countertops, and all other decor. But naming our new dog was a bigger deal to me than just deciding on colors or decor. Names have depth, meaning, and carry weight behind them.

As we sat there, I kept my eyes on her, observing her body language, trying to gauge what she was thinking. But I couldn't tell behind the poker face she was wearing. Another minute passed before Crystal finally spoke up. "I love it!"

Overjoyed with her response, I heard the theme song of *Gladiator* playing in my mind, just imagining our Maximus running around in a gladiator outfit.

We actually ended up buying him a custom-made gladiator outfit meant for a baby, which never fit him. Who would've thought clothes for babies and puppies weren't interchangeable? Today it's pinned up on our kitchen wall above his food and water bowls as a friendly reminder that some ideas are better left alone.

Crystal and I impatiently counted down the days until it was time to meet our Maximus. We arranged a meeting with the seller at a local restaurant parking lot, by the front door and in broad daylight. Call me paranoid, but you can never be too careful these days with scammers and people who have bad intentions.

Crystal and I waited by the restaurant's front door, excited yet nervous for the seller to arrive. We had never done this kind of thing before. It's not an everyday occurrence that you meet a stranger in a parking lot, hand them cash, they give you an animal, and you both go your separate ways, never to speak again.

It felt like we'd waited forever before realizing it was 2:42 p.m., twelve minutes past the agreed meet-up time. As I began to wonder if we were being duped, a rusted dark green Jeep zoomed through the restaurant parking lot, pulling up into a space next to where we were standing. Crystal and I were standing about ten feet away when the Jeep door opened, and out came an older woman wearing a stained shirt, oversized sweatpants, and open-toe sandals with torn socks, holding a half-smoked cigarette in her hand.

"Is y'all picking' up a dawg?" Her southernness and years of chain-smoking could be heard in her raspy voice.

Crystal quietly spoke up. "Yeah... that's us."

The lady guided us to the opposite side of her Jeep. We stood close as she opened the door to grab Maximus. My excitement nearly died as I was forced to hold my breath, in order to not puke, from the overwhelming stench of cigarette smoke and rotten fast food I could see molding on her floorboard.

The lady handed Maximus to me as Crystal gave her the cash. I adored him, but through no fault of his own, I noticed he smelled just as putrid as her Jeep did.

I held Maximus up in front of me, looked right into his eyes, and whispered, "I can't wait to give you a bath. We're gonna get you nice and clean tonight." Apparently I had never learned to use my "inside voice."

Hearing this, the lady turned around and gave me the death stare like something was wrong with *my* sense of smell. And then she totally snapped.

"I done already gave him a bath before I came up here. That's a fact! I reckon ya don't believe me?"

My wife and I glanced at each other, exchanging the "Oh shit" look as we shared this awkward moment. Realizing we'd never see this stranger again and not wanting the situation to escalate, I ended our meeting abruptly.

"Um, okay . . . well, thanks for the dog. Take care."

Crystal and I spun around and bolted toward our car, not daring to look back at the lady, whom I'd clearly offended. It was a cold exit, but necessary, as the lady was getting heated. I wasn't going to stand there and argue with a stranger, or anyone for that matter, in a parking lot.

Mark Twain is thought to have said, "Never argue with a fool, onlookers may not be able to tell the difference."

I've held onto this insight for years, living it out, which has certainly brought more peace into my life, preventing unnecessary drama.

After arriving home that afternoon, Crystal and I gave Maximus a bath, ensuring he smelled fresh like he deserved. We didn't do much for the rest of that evening, letting time pass us by as we watched Maximus play with his new toys until he finally fell asleep, worn out from the day's events. Crystal and I stayed up late that evening, laying in bed raving about our new pup and planning all the places we'd go together—the park, the beach, and any dog-friendly coffee shops. Day one with Maximus was truly a success in our eyes. And although he was quite adorable, this puppy would prove to be more than a handful for our household.

Chapter 14
Blaze

Before Crystal and I knew it, October 2018 had arrived—just a month since Maximus was welcomed into his new home. We basked in our new roles as dog parents, capturing every moment with him on our camera rolls, sharing them on social media, not stopping short of annoying our friends and followers. But we didn't care. We were excited and proud of our Maximus. But alongside those wonderful moments with our new pup were a fair share of challenges that we hadn't foreseen.

This was our hope, that this crazy idea would move our world forward once again, restoring some sort of normalcy to our day-to-day lives. It would certainly be a bold move, but one that we feared could be disastrous, with two dogs destroying our house instead of one. And what if they didn't get along? What if they hurt each other? Would adding another dog to the mix *really* be the answer here?

These concerns were overwhelming, reminding us we were in way over our heads. Regardless of our doubts, we had to act soon and do something to save our sanity along with the house.

Crystal and I understood accidents in the house would happen with Maximus when it came to potty training. We also expected him to chew up our shoes and clothes—for the record, he fully met our expectations there. But one thing we didn't consider was *why* he was originally named "Blaze." Remember earlier when I said that names have depth, meaning, and carry weight behind them? Well, I should've asked the lady who sold him to us for more details about his name. Soon I'd learn the hard way, right from first-hand experience.

It was a Friday, our busiest day of the week at work, and I was running late. The night before, I had placed my washed clothes in the dryer and walked away, forgetting to actually hit the start button. When I woke up the next morning, discovering my clothes were still wet in the dryer, I only had two options: be late for work or show up on time wearing wet clothes. I certainly wasn't going to wear wet clothes, but I also wasn't going to be later than I needed to be.

In a rush, I got ready and started making a sandwich that I planned on eating during the commute to work. Before I could finish, my phone rang with a call I couldn't ignore, nearly in sync with the dryer timer buzzing. Fumbling around between taking that important call and getting dressed, I was completely distracted, leaving my half-made sandwich unattended at the edge of the kitchen counter.

Once I was off the phone and ready to leave the house, I made my way back to the kitchen to finish making my sandwich, only to find it was gone.

It didn't take long for me to realize what had just occurred. I looked for Maximus and found him on the couch, sitting there as if he were completely innocent, although the peanut butter on his snout told a different story. Now, I was really late and nearly starving, as I hadn't eaten since lunch the day before. Moving like I was a finalist on *Top Chef* I quickly threw together another sandwich before heading out. With the sandwich in one hand and car keys in the other, I walked over to the front door to leave—and that's when it happened. Like a thief in the night, Maximus leaped up, snatched the sandwich right out of my hand, and bolted away. I chased him, but couldn't come close to matching his speed and wit. I tripped over myself as Maximus outmaneuvered me, bouncing from couch to couch and table to table in a magnificent display of parkour.

In a matter of minutes, I had given up, realizing I'd never catch him. And even if I did, what would I do? Take the sandwich back and eat it? As I stood there catching my breath, I shook my head and couldn't help but smile, realizing how I'd wasted time chasing him instead of just making another sandwich. I left the house and worked the rest of that day with hunger pangs, thanks to "Blaze."

Crystal and I got better at protecting our food from Maximus but didn't always succeed. At times, he proved clever in his ways, scanning counters, and using his charm and agility to get an extra meal that wasn't meant for him. But despite his mischievous ways, we loved our Maximus.

Over the next few weeks, we discovered he was an exceptional learner, who ended up mastering potty training faster than any dog I'd ever known. He also kept us on our toes with his high-octane energy, always initiating playtime, whether or not we were ready. Maximus was everything we needed in our lives.

While at work, we'd leave Maximus in his kennel, awaiting the moment we'd see him again. As the work hours became longer, I questioned the quality of life we were giving him. He was an individual, and being locked up in a kennel all day was no life that any living being deserves. In our attempt to honor this conviction, moving forward we decided to let Maximus roam the house in a small closed-off space while we were gone.

When we arrived home after his first day in this new limited freedom, we seriously questioned if we'd made a mistake. The floors were covered in pee and poo, which was completely out of his character, considering he rarely had accidents in the house. And to our complete shock, whatever flooring wasn't covered in his excrement was destroyed. Somehow, through sheer willpower, Maximus had been able to peel up and chew through the laminate flooring all the way to the concrete foundation! Although this was extremely frustrating and would be costly to repair, we didn't want to put him back in his kennel. Our conscience wouldn't allow it. Crystal and I stayed the course for another month, hoping it would just get better, but things actually just got worse—the floors, and now the walls, along with their baseboards, were slowly being chewed away. Something had to change soon.

"I think he's just anxious and lonely," Crystal suggested, as we were cleaning up another disaster that Maximus had left.

Ultimately, we realized leaving him alone for hours on end would not work. We also weren't going to keep him in his kennel all day either. Caught in a conundrum, Crystal and I were unsure of what to do.

We painfully thought through this predicament for weeks, constantly frustrated, not knowing how much longer we could continue down this path. It was exhausting on every level imaginable. And then, seemingly out of nowhere, a solution finally came to mind. To this day, I'm uncertain how we arrived at this conclusion, as one little dog was more than enough to handle. But we paddled around the idea of getting Maximus a friend to keep him company—a truly radical concept for us at the time.

In an interview discussing her memoir, *The Country Under My Skin*, Gioconda Belli commented, "The world has always gone forward when people have dared to have crazy ideas."

This was our hope, that this crazy idea would move our world forward once again, restoring some sort of normalcy to our day-to-day lives. It would certainly be a bold move, but one that we feared could be disastrous, with two dogs destroying our house instead of one. And what if they didn't get along? What if they hurt each other? Would adding another dog to the mix really be the answer here?

These concerns were overwhelming, reminding us we were in way over our heads. Regardless of our doubts, we had to act soon and do something to save our sanity along with the house.

Chapter 15

Mister Max

In December 2018, the search for Maximus's new friend officially began. Similar to our previous dog search, Crystal used the same site to find our next pup. Together we scrolled through the pictures and stopped when we came across a dog who caught our attention, named "Mister Max." He was a beautiful Morkie with white and copper hair, the runt of his litter, born a week before Maximus. We were excited that they were essentially the same age and could grow up together, but we weren't thrilled with the idea of having two dogs whose names were that similar. And as before, we went through the naming process once again.

"We need to go with a theme," Crystal insisted. "We have Maximus from *Gladiator*, so we should name this one..."

"Leonidas? Gerard Butler's character from *300*," I interrupted out of excitement.

She briefly paused, really putting some thought into it. "Hmm, doesn't sound quite right."

I sighed in agreement, "Yeah, you're right, way too many syllables for a dog name."

Another moment passed before it came to me, "Okay, I think I've got it! Who's the most famous gladiator of all time? Spartacus!"

Crystal's eyes widened as she nodded her head in approval. "Maximus and Spartacus... it has a ring to it. I love it!"

A few days later, we met the seller at our local animal hospital, unsure of what to expect because of our experience when we picked up Maximus. To our relief, the meeting turned out to be pretty normal. We gave the lady cash, and she handed over Spartacus, exchanging a few friendly words before going our separate ways.

When I first held Spartacus, I realized he was the polar opposite of Maximus—quiet and timid. He also didn't enjoy being touched or cuddled like Maximus. I quickly discovered this after he'd snapped at me for getting too close.

Throughout the week, Crystal and I noticed he was displaying subtle, but troublesome, signs of neglect and abuse. Spartacus was very protective of his food, possibly because he was the runt and had missed out on some meals. Watching him eat, you'd think he hadn't eaten in years and that the food in front of him was the last meal available on planet Earth. His aggression progressively got worse, not only toward us, but toward Maximus. This made us fear for Maximus's safety, because he was a kind, trusting, and sociable dog. The dreaded scenario, which we rehearsed in our heads a thousand times, was that Spartacus would interpret Maximus's playful demeanor as an invasion of his personal space and attack. We were completely lost, unsure of what to do.

Additionally, his previous owner had led us to believe Spartacus had been potty trained. This was not the case, having several accidents a day no matter what we tried—puppy pads, training bells, you name it. Unlike Maximus, he was a slow learner. The accidents weren't our primary concern though. We were more alarmed that whenever Spartacus would have an accident in the house, he'd cower in fear, shaking, as if he thought his life was in danger. This sight broke our hearts.

Marianne Williamson, the founder of Project Angel Food, reminds us, "Love is what we are born with. Fear is what we learn."

The very thought that someone had instilled fear in him for having accidents in the house was devastating. Regardless, Spartacus didn't deserve to live like that; nobody does. *Had someone hit him?* I'll never know.

Although we demonstrated patience and love with Spartacus, I'd be dishonest if I said we didn't think about re-homing him, not because of the accidents, but because of his aggression. One evening after he lashed out against Maximus, we sat in our bedroom as Crystal was in tears. "I don't know if we can keep doing this. Maximus could be in danger without us here."

The hardships Spartacus was putting us through made us question whether bringing him into our family had been the wrong decision. Through our frustrations, negative thoughts surfaced toward him:

Why can't you just act like a normal dog? And even worse, *why can't you be more like Maximus?*

Despite the hopelessness of the situation, the tide would soon turn in our favor. A few days after we had considered re-homing him, I sat on the couch flipping through an old photo album. As I was turning the pages, reminiscing down memory lane, a photograph of Lexi as a puppy grabbed my attention. I couldn't help but think about what she'd done for me, looking past all my faults and instead seen me for who I could become—a demonstration of true love. *Why wasn't I doing the same for Spartacus?* This thought convicted me to my core, compelling me to reevaluate the condition of my heart. I wondered about his past and what he could've endured as a young pup that had caused all of this behavior. I then viewed Spartacus through a lens of compassion... that changed everything.

Over the next few weeks, we pushed through loving Spartacus with every bit of our souls. When we endured love a little longer, he became a completely different dog, as if we had pressed a magical button. But it wasn't magic. Spartacus's confidence in himself was slowly restored, along with his capacity to trust, all because we *chose* to love him relentlessly. He no longer cowered in fear whenever he had an accident in the house, nor did he continue snapping at Crystal, me, or

Maximus. To our delight, Spartacus and Maximus even began playing together, becoming inseparable, as we had originally hoped. His transformation before our very eyes was something beautiful that I hope everyone gets to experience one day.

Crystal and I were thrilled to witness Spartacus thriving in his new life with us. We found so much joy in watching his friendship with Maximus blossom. And although we were extremely grateful to have progressed this far with him, something had to be done about the frequency of his accidents. It was happening so often that it took an act of faith to clean up Spartacus's mess, nearly using an entire roll of paper towels a day. This became expensive rather quickly, forcing me to get a monthly subscription for paper towels in order to save some money.

Despite the challenges, we found Spartacus was a great listener, and didn't want to give up on him—truly believing he had the capacity to be potty trained. We tried everything; from books and podcasts to online trainings, but *nothing* worked. After several failed attempts, Crystal and I nearly resigned ourselves to the idea of budgeting paper towels into our monthly expenses in perpetuity. After exhausting every possible option and almost giving up, one very small glimmer of hope became visible in the distance. It was an idea that struck me; a long shot that was so crazy I thought it might just work.

That night, when we let the dogs outside to use the bathroom, I walked out there with them, following Spartacus around the yard, encouraging him to go. He did his usual thing, sniffing the ground around him, but refusing to go before running back inside. As he ran toward the back door, I called him, and he returned in curiosity.

Trotting closer, he sat in the grass and looked at me. "Spartacus, sit, boy. I need you to watch."

In a desperate attempt to potty train him, I did what all great leaders do—led by example. With all the chips on the table, this was going to be my final stand. I was *all in*.

Scanning the back yard, I turned my head to the left and back to the right, making sure we were truly alone. Seeing the coast was clear, I pulled down the elastic of my sweat pants, slightly with my thumb, just enough to clear the stream. Then I did it... pissed in my own yard like I was a nine-year-old on a family camping trip.

Crystal walked onto the porch just in time to witness my moment of glory.

"Kerk, what are you doing? Are you out of your mind?"

"Nope, just out of better ideas," I shouted, still focused, trying to finish up what I considered to be my official dog-training certification.

With genuine concern in her voice, she tried to reason with me. "Kerk, the neighbors can see you."

"It's dark outside, and we have a fence. If they peek over it, it's their problem."

I could tell exactly what she was thinking as she shook her head in disbelief, giving me that distinct look—the same one Michael Scott from *The Office* always gave Toby: *"Why are you the way that you are?"*

I wasn't certain of where the HOA stood on this issue, but I felt I had every right to pee in my own vinyl-fenced backyard while potty training my dog. As I finished, letting the elastic band on my sweatpants snap back up into position, I noticed Spartacus sniffing around where I had just gone. I'm not certain what he was thinking, but in nothing short of a miracle, he began to pee. My crazy idea had *actually* worked.

From that day forward, Spartacus continued using the bathroom outside, and I was eventually able to cancel our monthly paper towel subscription on Amazon. But I must confess that every now and then, I find myself outside with Spartacus, tending to nature's call, reinforcing what he'd learned on that one winter night—that I was willing to do anything to demonstrate my love for him, even if that meant peeing together in the backyard.

Chapter 16
A Lesson in Love

December 29, 2018 seemed to be an ordinary day. I was at work taking care of the items on my never-ending to-do list and waiting for my time to punch out. As I ran around putting out "fires," quickly maneuvering my team to solve the issues, hands completely full, I couldn't answer my phone that I felt vibrating in my pocket. In my position at the company, it wasn't unusual for me to receive several calls and texts a day.

By midmorning, business had calmed down, just enough for me to take a quick break and scan through unread notifications on my phone. I was alarmed to see several missed calls and texts from my parents. Usually they'd call or text, but rarely both, so I knew something wasn't right.

As I headed toward the back office, I scrolled through some of the other texts before reading my parents' message. I opened the office door and sat down on the only chair I could see—it was made of hard plastic and had no back, built for productivity, not comfort. Unlocking my phone, I understood exactly why my parents had both called and texted me. Their message read, "Lexi's gone. I'm sorry, son."

Below the text were a few pictures of Lexi in her final moments, eyes closed and Dad's hand resting on her as she took her last breath. I felt my heart stop as my world shattered and time stood still, waiting for me to accept its harsh reality. I completely lost it. Sobbing with my head pressed against that cold desk, tears soaked the papers below me, making the ink bleed. I let out an agonizing wail, yet it wasn't enough to express my grief.

Crystal, who worked with me, came in the office, and found me completely inconsolable.

"Kerk, what happened? What's wrong?" I heard the heightened concern in her voice, as she hadn't seen me like this before.

I sat there trying to gather myself without facing her, hiding my swollen eyes and the snot running down my face.

"Lexi. She's dead."

Crystal hugged me from behind, trying to pick up the broken pieces. She held me for a few minutes before someone tried to open the office door. Crystal jumped up and blocked them from entering, shooing them away and giving me the privacy I needed. She remained outside standing guard, letting everyone know the office was off-limits.

Almost an hour later, completely drained, my tears dried up, and rational thought returned to me once again. Despite the dread I'd felt since Thanksgiving, I wasn't surprised this day had arrived.

A few weeks earlier my parents had texted, letting me know Lexi was swiftly declining, and for her own good, they'd need to put her down soon. They even asked me if I wanted to come home to see her one last time. And, for selfish reasons, I declined.

I wasn't ready to say goodbye; I wasn't strong enough for that. I knew my heart wouldn't be able to handle seeing Lexi lying there, so frail, preparing to leave her earthly body. I should've been there. That's one decision I'll always regret.

While I had the option of leaving work, I chose not to in order to keep my mind off of the fact that I had lost a piece of myself forever. I finished out the work day, hoping for some normalcy amid all the emotions overflowing within me.

Arriving home that evening, I unlocked the front door, stepped into the house and sat on the floor, breaking down all over again. At that very moment, Maximus and Spartacus sprinted to me and gave me the soft landing I needed, licking away my tears, reminding me I wasn't alone in my grief.

In an article, "The Gift of a Great Dog," Meghan Daum writes, "There will always be that dog that no dog will replace, the dog that will make you cry even when it's been gone for more years than it could ever have lived. I have now had that dog. That is at once the most beautiful and most awful thing in the world."

Lexi undoubtedly was that dog for me.

That day was the end of an era. I desperately wanted to go back to being seventeen, even if that meant living through all that hell again, just to hold Lexi once more. Although I knew that was impossible, it didn't stop me from reminiscing about those beautiful moments we shared, which made losing her even more devastating.

Today, Lexi's pink bandanna hangs on the living room wall, along with her collar and the last picture we took together. Most times, I smile while looking at it, overwhelmed with gratitude to have experienced her love. But other times, I lose it, completely falling apart. Although I live with the regret of not being there for Lexi as she crossed the Rainbow Bridge, that selfish decision changed me for the better. From that day forward, I committed to becoming a better friend to others, using compassion to look past their faults. But more importantly, to see them not only as they are, but who they could become—a lesson in love I learned from my sweet Lexi.

Chapter 17

In the Passenger Seat

During the summer of 2019, life had returned mostly to normal after months grieving Lexi. Although it had been nearly half a year since her passing, I still didn't feel much better. Loss is something I truly believe you never "get over." You just learn to live with the grief, like an undesirable roommate you hope you'll never see, but know it's inevitable. It lingers inside of us, waiting to resurface—one look at that picture, the scent of that fragrance, hearing that certain phrase, or driving past that place is all it takes for us to be returned into grief's painful grip. All we can do is force ourselves to smile once again and live on, even if we don't feel ready. And that's exactly what I did.

In this season of life, Crystal and I embraced the hustle culture. Completely consumed by our careers, we missed birthdays, weddings, and other social gatherings. We embodied the "work hard, play hard" mantra, carelessly spending our money on whatever we desired. We had finally "arrived" in life, or so I thought.

On one particular afternoon that June, I was excited for Crystal as we shopped for her dream car—a new black and red Jeep. The year before, I had picked up my dream car from a dealership in Atlanta, driving home in a $130,000 Dodge Viper GTC. The sound of its 8.4L V10 engine, alongside its sheer performance, made for an exhilarating experience each and every time I sat behind the wheel. But even owning a car like that wasn't enough to satisfy the emptiness within me that longed for a more purposeful life. In hindsight, buying that car turned out to be very expensive therapy.

Later that week, while Crystal was working, I drove to the dealership to sign for the Jeep. Upon arrival, I noticed the salesperson was busy with another client. Being in the service industry for the past seventeen years, I understood that interrupting their discussion may not serve me well in negotiating a lower price. So strategically, I decided to wait outside on the dingy plastic bench by the front door. Suddenly, my stomach reminded me I hadn't eaten all day, so I rose and hurried to my car to grab the bagged lunch I hadn't eaten at work.

Returning, I caught a glimpse of someone who would unexpectedly change my life forever. In my peripheral vision was a puppy, no more than eight weeks old, laying under the shade of the canopy, seeking refuge from the unforgiving South Georgia heat. With one glance at his malnourished body, I could easily see that it had been days or maybe weeks since his last meal.

Several people saw the puppy as they passed by the entrance, one by one, even stepping over him, as if his existence didn't matter. Looking a little closer, I noticed a festering wound on his face.

Watching a little longer, I wondered what was going through his mind on that first night—the one where he realized he was completely alone, without a friend in the world. What a burden that must have been to carry.

His pleas for help and squealing for someone to care was gut-wrenching. The sight of him suffering, within the presence of so many, made me absolutely sick to my stomach. I *had* to do something.

Standing, I walked toward him and knelt down as his weary eyes met mine. The gaze of his innocence awakened something within my soul that words could never explain. I could not resist him, nor did I want to. In that moment, somehow I became more human, arriving to this divine appointment that destined me to answer his question—one that I knew all too well.

Am I worthy of love?

When I reached out to touch him, to further examine his condition, his eyes lit up as if he knew I held the answer to his question. Brushing my hand through his precious black coat, the fleas that were on him began to jump on me. I quickly slapped them off my arms unfazed, completely focused on this puppy's well-being.

I returned to the bench to get the rest of my lunch for him but when I turned around, he was not where I'd left him. For a moment I panicked, until I realized with relief that he'd followed me and was lying at my feet.

I fed him what was left of my lunch and contemplated the next move. Although I already knew what had to be done, I had my reservations. I'd never taken home a stray animal before—a thousand thoughts rushed through my mind.

Who was I to do this?

What am I supposed to do once I get him home?

Am I keeping him forever?

I wrestled with those thoughts as more onlookers passed by. "So sad," one lady said distressingly, "Somebody ought to do something about this."

I paused for a moment, letting those words soak in, which triggered something within me and gave me the assurance I needed to follow my heart.

I am somebody.

After that epiphany, I heard the salesperson finally call my name. "Kerk, you ready?" To her disappointment, I politely told her I'd have to come back another day as I was more concerned about the puppy.

Crouching down on the pavement, I looked into his eyes. "All right friend, are you ready to go?" Without hesitation, he followed me to the car.

I opened the door and he jumped right in and laid patiently in the passenger seat, staring at me and waiting for what was next. Smiling, I gave him an ear rub and cracked a joke.

"You know, there aren't many stray dogs who get to sit inside of a Viper? Heck, there are some humans I wouldn't let into this car. They'd be totally jealous of you."

From the look on his face, I could tell my attempt at humor wasn't very effective, as he clearly didn't understand one word I had said. But, I truly believed that he felt my intentions. For his sake, I thought humor would bring some lightheartedness into the situation. But looking back, perhaps it was more for me to distract my mind from the suffering he had endured in his brief existence. His trauma, his scars, the hope for redemption—sitting right next to me in the passenger seat was the story of all of us.

When we arrived home, I opened the passenger door for him and he hopped out, following me into the garage. I grabbed the spare dog bowl, filling it with water, and set it down for him to drink. He hesitantly approached, sniffed the bowl, approved, then gulped it all down as I walked over to hook up an old hose that was rarely used.

Overhearing the commotion, Maximus and Spartacus began scratching at the garage door from inside the house, barking, wondering why I was home and not with them. Out of concern for the weak puppy, I decided not to let them outside, unsure of how they'd react.

After he lapped up all the water, I walked him out toward the driveway, closer to the hose.

"Are you ready, boy? I'm gonna give you a bath now."

Although it was scorching hot outside, he didn't like the water—not one bit. He sabotaged my attempts to bathe him with his frantic movements and high-pitched yelps.

"It's okay, boy," I kept reassuring him in the softest of tones, "You're gonna feel a lot better when we're finished."

He stopped resisting when he realized his efforts were futile against my tenacity to wash every flea off of his body. I marched on the warpath searching, scrubbing, rinsing, and repeating. My strategy reflected General William Tecumseh Sherman's policy of total war—one where those vermin understood that "war is hell." This was the measure of my resolve.

I don't think I'd ever been so thorough in bathing an animal—or myself, if we're being honest. With every flea I washed off his body, I became more and more his liberator, triumphantly undoing the wrongs done to him.

Something miraculous was blossoming in plain sight. This creature was no longer a vagabond, an outcast, or someone's burden. He, who had once been an afterthought, was being restored to the original version of himself, reclaiming his identity that had been lost. Washing him, I realized I was unveiling the answer to the question that his heart desired to know.

Am I worthy of love?

Every piece of myself I gave to him on that day responded to that question—not aloud, but through the invisible fellowship of our souls.

After the bath, I wrapped him in a beach towel and gently dried him off. I held him so close to me I could feel our hearts beating together in perfect harmony. Our eyes met, as he cracked a smile, embodying words from Fyodor Dostoevsky's novel, *The Brothers Karamazov:* "Joy untroubled."

Without a doubt, this puppy knew he was worthy of love. This extraordinary moment is one that I often think of and will never forget. I was fortunate enough to capture it on camera; it's been the background image on my phone ever since. For a second, I saw Lexi in him and was taken back to the seventeen-year-old me. Maybe it was the way he looked at me, or perhaps it was his dark coat—or maybe it was just being in the presence of pure innocence that took me down memory lane. I couldn't help but wonder if he was going to be somebody's Lexi, leading them to their redemption. Right there in my garage, holding him, I sobbed uncontrollably, overwhelmed with joy that he was finally redeemed.

At the end of my days, when I have physically passed from this life into the next, if there's any talk about my legacy, I earnestly hope that people will recall this moment. To give one the gift of discovering who they are and who they could become, to infuse them with a sense of their true worth, to walk the path with one toward their moment of redemption; I don't know what more we could hope to experience in our lives. What accomplishment could *ever* be greater?

I continued to hold him, watching as he fell asleep in my arms, finally knowing love. But sadly, I knew our journey together would have to end. Crystal and I didn't have the capacity to take care of another dog, especially the way he deserved. In good conscience, I had to find him another home.

Shortly afterward, Crystal arrived home from a long workday. Getting out of her car, she saw me holding the puppy and didn't even ask about the Jeep. I explained to her what had happened, and she was understanding, as she's always been. After filling her in on my intentions for the puppy, she left for the store to get supplies while I attempted to find his forever home.

Out of ignorance, I made the mistake of listing him as "free." Later, I would learn this is strongly discouraged in order to deter ill-intentioned people from snatching up these vulnerable creatures and using them as bait in illegal dog-fighting arenas or subjecting them to other unspeakable cruelty. My natural instinct was to list him with no fees to expedite the process, and it never occurred to me that he could fall into the wrong hands. If you find yourself needing to re-home an animal, please do not make the same mistake as me.

Utilizing our network, within an hour, I found him a great family who needed a companion for their own dog. They ended up naming him Gunner.

Crystal returned just in time as Gunner's new family pulled into our driveway in their gray SUV. Sandy, from Facebook, who was even more pleasant in person, got out of her car to greet Gunner. She was all that I'd hoped for, adoring him at first sight. It was a bittersweet moment watching Sandy hold him, knowing that my new four-legged friend would be leaving soon. Crystal handed her a kennel and leash as I exchanged a heartfelt goodbye with Gunner, kissing him on his head one last time. I released him as Sandy sat him in the passenger seat, keeping him wrapped in the towel I'd used earlier. She got back into her SUV, shut the door, and waved at us before disappearing into the dusk, taking Gunner to his new home.

Although I didn't go home with a new Jeep that day, I left the dealership with a lot more than I could've imagined. Looking back, I never became the hero that the thirteen-year-old me wanted to be—the courageous Maximus from *Gladiator*. It took twenty more years to discover that I would become something greater than any of my childhood aspirations. In a moment that I'll hold on to forever, a once wandering soul, who found refuge in my arms, gazed at me as if I were his hero. And for me, that will always be enough.

Chapter 18
Caught in the Middle

After Gunner's rescue, I couldn't help but constantly think of him, wondering how he was adapting to his new life. I took comfort in knowing he was in excellent hands with Sandy and her family. To my surprise, Sandy wanted to keep in touch and even schedule meet-ups so I could see Gunner regularly. I never asked her to do this, but it was certainly welcome. All seemed right with the world... that is, until my life radically changed after receiving a text.

While I know this to be true today, I wasn't so certain of that back then. As much as my heart was thrusting me into my destiny, my head was yanking me even further away, taking the upper-hand in the civil war within me. My yearning heart just wasn't enough to compel me to take action. It was apparent that I needed something truly substantial, along the lines of a miracle, to push me toward making the impossible happen and ultimately become who I was meant to be.

June 21, 2019 is a day I'll never forget. I had just finished up another day at work, ready to head home, and was walking through the parking lot toward my car. Just as I opened the door, my phone vibrated in my pocket. I got in my car and pulled out my phone, noticing there was a text notification from Sandy. Excited to hear from her again after nearly a week, I hurried to read the message.

"Hey, Kerk. I'm so sorry to have to tell you this, but Gunner passed away. We did everything we could to save him, taking him to the vet countless times. He was having seizures and wasn't eating. We found out he had parvo, two types of worms, and an intestinal infection. We did everything we could to save him."

Time stood still as I sat there, overcome with shock, body numb, unable to process what I'd just read. My heart raced as my lungs struggled for air, choking on the heaviness of the horrible news. Unable to feel my fingers, the phone slipped out of my hand, tumbling from the seat to the floorboard. It felt like an eternity had passed before the shock wore off and the grief took over.

Nearly an hour later, I was finally able to gather myself enough to drive home safely. I walked in the front door and let my body fall onto the couch, hoping it was sturdy enough to hold the anguish that weighed me down. Maximus and Spartacus did their best to comfort me, licking away my tears, nuzzling up next to me, and helping to carry my heartache. Crystal arrived home shortly afterward and sat with me, as I ugly-cried right in her lap, eventually exhausting myself and falling asleep.

Over the next few weeks and months, Gunner's passing affected me more than I could've imagined. Several times I attempted to put it behind me and move forward, but it wasn't that simple. The more I pushed Gunner into the back of my mind, the more empty and unresolved I felt. No matter how much I tried, it was impossible for me to stop thinking about the day I had rescued Gunner and how rewarding it had been.

It quickly became apparent to me that the life I was living was shallow and meaningless, in constant pursuit of material wealth, which didn't satisfy and was *never* enough. This all changed the day I listened to my heart, which was telling me I needed to help more animals like Gunner. This frightened me because I was unsure of how to actually do this. Yet at the same time, the idea of helping animals invigorated my soul. I couldn't deny my heart had discovered its purpose.

My first instinct was to donate money to nonprofit organizations that could help animals in need. I was thrilled to think I could impact the life of an animal by supporting one of these groups. Following my heart, I did some research and found a local organization I wanted to support. I'll always remember the November day when I visited their website and clicked on the donate button. As I looked at my checking account to see what I could give, this idea I had to help animals began to look grim—there was no money to give. Crystal and I had carelessly spent all the money we'd made on materialistic items that essentially meant nothing. And now, there was a cause I cared so much about without the resources to help. Ashamed could not begin to explain how I felt. I didn't know what else to do, so I gave up, convincing myself that I wasn't meant to help animals.

Before I knew it, February 2020 had arrived. It had been three months since I'd lost hope that I could help animals like Gunner. Although I had mentally given up on that idea, my heart relentlessly implored me to try again every day since visiting that nonprofit site. Of course nothing had changed financially within that time frame, so I wasn't sure what I was supposed to do.

Trying to think outside the box, I sat on this a little longer, and that's when it struck me—the craziest idea I ever had in my life. I thought perhaps I could write a book about Gunner and donate the proceeds to an animal rescue organization. One glaring problem with that plan was that I didn't know the first thing about writing a book or telling stories. I was just an ordinary guy, whose heart desired to help animals. Yet, in my own mind, I believed I was a far cry from being qualified.

Who was I to do something like this?

As absurd as that sounded, days later, another idea formed that was even more ridiculous.

Why don't I just start a nonprofit organization to help animals?

Writing a book was one thing, but starting a nonprofit organization was a whole other level of naïvety for me. While these ideas were thrilling, the more research I did, the more I realized I was in over my head. The upfront cost for both ventures was staggering, especially considering that I didn't have any extra money lying around. It was also overwhelming to think about the time investment that would be required. Focusing on these obstacles, I found myself back at square one without a realistic plan and, even worse, no hope of helping animals at all.

I was caught in the middle of a raging civil war between fear and faith. My head and heart were contending against one another for control—my head logically telling me that this was impossible and my heart reassuring me that I was bigger than my fears. Where was I to go from here?

Days passed as I continued to struggle, being tugged at from both sides. Even through all the noise, I knew what I *should* do—follow my heart. But the idea of writing a book and starting a nonprofit organization seemed so far-fetched. At best, it was wishful thinking, a mere fairy tale.

A few months ago, my friend Lauren, the founder of Fawn's Fortress, told me, "Truth is we are all full of magic when we want to do something. We have all at one point made the impossible happen."

While I know this to be true today, I wasn't so certain of that back then. As much as my heart was thrusting me into my destiny, my head was yanking me even further away, taking the upper-hand in the civil war within me. My yearning heart just wasn't enough to compel me to take action. It was apparent that I needed something truly substantial, along the lines of a miracle, to push me toward making the impossible happen and ultimately become who I was meant to be.

Chapter 19
This Dream

In March 2020, I was still wrestling with the ideas of writing a book and starting a nonprofit organization. I had every reason not to do so, beginning with the fact that I was already buried in my very full-time job, leading a multi-million-dollar business. Additionally, these ventures were going to cost me a lot of money and time that I didn't have. Lastly, I had no experience in doing either. These ideas terrified me even more as I thought about them through a logical lense. But my heart kept urging me to take the leap into the unknown and figure things out along the way.

One evening as I went to bed completely exhausted from work and my inability to make a decision, I did the only thing I knew to do. I prayed, practically giving God an ultimatum.

"God, if I'm supposed to write this book and start this nonprofit, I need a clear sign. I won't make a move until then."

That night, I had a dream I'll never forget. In this dream I was seventeen again, yet I had a total awareness of the future and everything that had happened in my life. I was standing completely still in my childhood room, the same one that had haunted me for so long. But it was different this time. It wasn't dark. The room was bursting with light from all directions, but not so bright that I couldn't keep my eyes open. It was enchanting, a breathtaking sight. Surrounding me was an overwhelming presence of tranquility that words could not fully explain. I stared at the closed door, uncertain about why I was there—only understanding that I was waiting for something to happen.

Then the door swung open, and I could see an even brighter light in the distance coming from miles away. Gazing into this path of light, in awe of its beauty, I saw a small, unrecognizable figure approaching me, but I wasn't frightened. As it got closer, the light became so radiant that the figure disappeared into its luminosity. For a second, I wondered what had happened to the figure, and that's when I felt a familiar sensation brushing up against my leg. When I looked down, I nearly lost my breath—it was Lexi.

I immediately burst into tears, holding her and not wanting to let go as she licked my face. Her fur was as dark as I had remembered, and she was no longer in an aged, frail body. She was young again. I sobbed, telling Lexi how much I missed her and how I was sorry for not being there during her last moments on Earth. Somehow, during all of this, I understood she was being taken care of and was at peace. Then, to my dismay, she disappeared from my arms almost as quickly as she had arrived. I turned around in a panic, searching for her, not knowing where she had gone. In my desperation to find her, I shouted, "Lexi, where are you? Don't leave me! Please. Don't go. I'll do anything. Just don't go."

I fell to my knees, sobbing, fearful I'd never see her again. Then, to my surprise, a voice spoke to me in what I can only describe as a majestic and divine tone. "Kerk, you were always enough."

After the voice spoke, the room disappeared, leaving me confused and standing in a blank white space. That's when the fourteen years of memories I had shared with Lexi flashed through my mind in an instant, no more than a few seconds, yet somehow I fully experienced each one again.

I woke up in tears, calling out for Lexi, which startled Crystal, waking her up. The dream had been so real, as if the supernatural and natural had collided to reunite me with my sweet Lexi. I'd never had a dream like that before nor since, even though I've prayed for it to happen again on more than a few occasions—especially on those harder days when I really miss her. Waking up the next morning, I knew without a doubt this dream was the sign I had asked for.

In late March 2020, I mustered enough courage to act on that dream, which led to much more than I ever imagined. Crystal and I became better stewards of our

resources, pursuing a new debt-free lifestyle, downsizing
our lives by trading in our Viper and Jeep for
much cheaper rides. Currently, both of us drive used
Hyundais. We also sold other possessions, eventually
getting rid of our house and moving into a smaller one
to save even more money. I used the extra funds to write
the book that you're reading today. And I'm proud to
say that all the net proceeds from this book will be
donated to the nonprofit I started in May 2020, The
Lexi's Legacy Foundation Inc.

The Lexi's Legacy Foundation is a 501(c)(3) nonprofit
organization committed to ending animal suffering
in every community by supporting local rescues and
sanctuaries. We just hit our one-year anniversary this
past May of 2021. Because of our faithful supporters,
we've helped raise over $100,000 in donations, services,
and building projects for over twenty animal rescue
organizations across the country. We're even beginning
to support animal rescue groups abroad. And in just one
year's time, we've helped change the lives of over *five
hundred* animals like Gunner, who now know love.

Looking back, those beautiful animals throughout
my life taught me so much about love, friendship, and
forgiveness. They've also shown me the magic in fully
embracing our own fairy tales—with all of their joys,
sorrows, love, and loss. And if we can bravely do this, no
matter where our story began, we surely can write the
ending.

In Neil Gaiman's novella, *Coraline*, he writes, "Fairy
tales are more than true: not because they tell us that

dragons exist, but because they tell us that dragons can be beaten."

Once upon a time, a dog named Chelsea walked into the life of a young boy, opening the window to his soul as he waited for Lexi, Maximus, Spartacus, and Gunner to arrive. These incredible dogs faithfully stood by the boy's side, helping him fight and slay the dragons in his life. And because of their love for him, that boy lived his own fairy tale.

I hope you enjoyed the book!

I love connecting with my readers. In case you missed it in the beginning, here's your invitation to join my private Facebook Reader Group:
facebook.com/groups/779562103953550

If you love feel-good stories with rescue animals, be sure to grab my other books for 50% off at
kerkmurray.com.

"Blaze" and "Mister Max" playing tug-of-war with a sock!

"In a moment that I'll hold on to forever, a once wandering soul, who found refuge in my arms, gazed at me as if I were his hero. And for me, that will always be enough."

Volunteers of the Lexi's Legacy Foundation donating blankets to the local humane society.

Maximus being a perfect gentleman
and Spartacus stealing kisses.

"Maximus The Wise."

Spartacus' birthday and cover debut.

Love this book? Don't forget to leave a review!

Help other readers discover *Pawprints On Our Hearts*. Every review matters and it matters a lot. It can be as short as one phrase to a few sentences. Wherever you bought this book, you can use this link to leave an honest review on Amazon, Goodreads, Bookbub, or your favorite retailer:

kerkmurray.com/products/review-pawprintsonourhearts

A Life You've Changed

Gladiator is one of the abused animals we've supported through the proceeds of this book. This sweet soul has endured suffering that no living being deserves. He was tortured and dumped, found abandoned with hundreds of cigarette burns on his body. But because of your generosity, we've been able to purchase critical supplies to help care for him in his healing journey. Today, Gladiator is on the mend, fully loved, and has found his forever home.

If I've learned anything from working in animal rescue and helping animals like Gladiator, it's that EVERY dollar matters!

Just because you can't do everything to help an animal doesn't mean you shouldn't do something.

If you're compelled by Gladiator's story and want to help more animals like him, please consider making a donation today.

Whether it's a monthly commitment for $1 or a one time donation, please take action today. Every dollar matters!

donorbox.org/everydollarmatters

Thank you so much for your support!

Giving Back

"Never underestimate the power of a small group of committed people to change the world. In fact, it is the only thing that ever has." —**Margaret Mead**

Kerk Murray's readers make a difference. Since the release of his memoir, *Pawprints On Our Hearts*, his generous readers have raised over $20,000 toward the care of abused animals through book proceeds as well as donations to the nonprofit he founded, *The Lexi's Legacy Foundation*. If you feel compelled to donate, you can do so right here:

donorbox.org/everydollarmatters

Here's a list of the animal rescue organizations that readers are supporting monthly through each Kerk Murray book sale:

1. 2nd Street Hooligans Rescue – California

2. Cuddly – California

3. Little Hill Sanctuary – California

4. Love Always Sanctuary – California

5. Sale Ranch Animal Sanctuary – California

6. The Shore Sanctuary – California

7. Viva Global Rescue – California

8. Road To Refuge Animal Sanctuary – Connecticut

9. The Riley Farm Sanctuary – Connecticut

10. Love Life Animal Rescue & Sanctuary – Florida

11. Live Freely Sanctuary – Florida

12. Operation Liberation – Florida

13. SAGE Sanctuary and Gardens for Education – Florida

14. Farm of the Free – Georgia

15. Humane Society Greater Savannah – Georgia

16. Roatan Rescue – Honduras

17. Ruby Slipper Goat Rescue – Kansas

18. Shy 38 Inc. – Kansas

19. Sowa Goat Sanctuary – Massachusetts

20. Angela's Ark – North Carolina

21. Billie's Buddies Animal Rescue – North Carolina

22. Fairytale Farm Animal Sanctuary – North Carolina

23. Blackbird Animal Refuge – New Jersey

24. Broncs and Buns Rescue and Rehab – New

Jersey

25. Fawn's Fortress – New Jersey

26. Happily Ever After Farm – New Jersey

27. Goats of Anarchy – New Jersey

28. Maddie & Sven's Rescue Sanctuary – New Jersey

29. Marley Meadows Animal Sanctuary – New Jersey

30. Old Fogey Farm – New Jersey

31. Rancho Relaxo – New Jersey

32. Runaway Farm – New Jersey

33. Troll House Animal Sanctuary – New Jersey

34. Wild Lands Wild Horse Fund – New Jersey

35. Happy Compromise Farm – New York

36. Sleepy Pig Farm Animal Sanctuary – New York

37. Woodstock Farm Sanctuary – New York

38. Enchanted Farm Sanctuary – Oregon

39. Harmony Farm Sanctuary – Oregon

40. Morningside Farm Sanctuary – Oregon

41. Charlie's Army Animal Rescue – Pennsylvania

42. Happy Heart Happy Home Farm & Rescue – Pennsylvania

43. The Philly Kitty Club – Pennsylvania

44. The Misfit Farm – Texas

45. Best Friends Animal Society – Utah

46. Harmony Farm Sanctuary and Wellness Center – Vermont

47. Off The Plate Farm Animal Sanctuary – Vermont

48. Gentle Acres Animal Haven – Virginia

49. Little Buckets Farm Sanctuary – Virginia

Visit Lexi On The Rainbow Bridge

Lexi always loved to make new friends! Be sure to sign her guestbook! You can visit her virtual memorial at

rainbowsbridge.com/residents/LEXI032/Resident.htm

Read More Books By KERK MURRAY

Bundle & Save 50% off on the entire *Hadley Cove Sweet Romance* series at kerkmurray.com.

Book 1: *Since the Day We Danced*
A wounded divorcee, a grieving widower, and the
rescue dog who shows them that second chances do
exist.

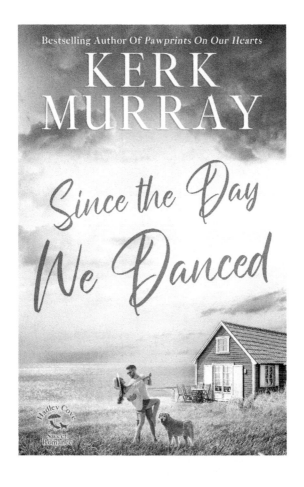

Book 2: *Since the Day We Fell*
Lisa never saw it coming—a failing
bed-and-breakfast, a rescue dog, and a second chance
at love.

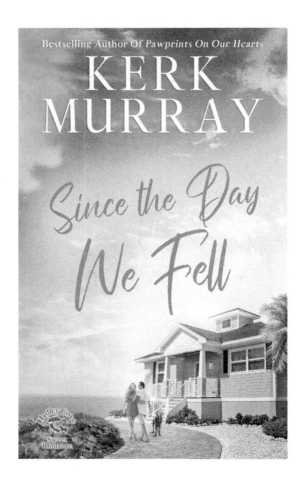

Book 3: *Since the Day We Kissed*
Kara thought her secret was safe—until her past
landed on her doorstep.

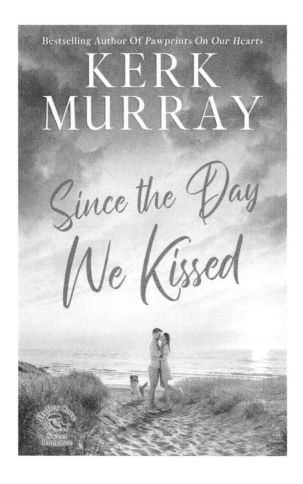

Book 4: *Since the Day We Wished*
Katie's secret wish, a lantern-lit night, and an
unexpected second chance at love.

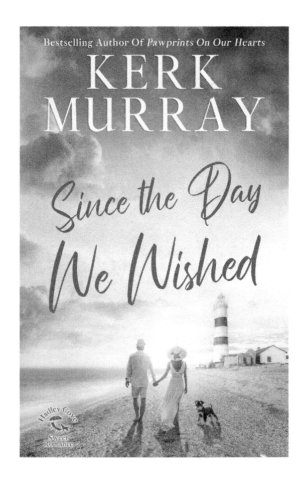

Book 5: *Since the Day We Left*
Wendi Parker never believed in love until she came back to Hadley Cove.

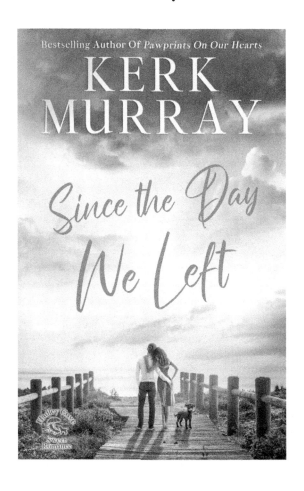

Prequel: *Since the Day We Promised*
**One summer wrote their story, but decades later, will
it bring them back into each other's arms?**

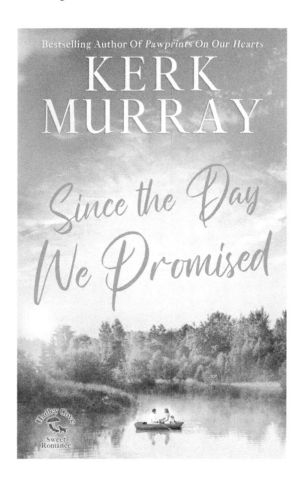

About the Author

Kerk Murray is the international bestselling and award-winning author of *Pawprints On Our Hearts* and the *Hadley Cove Sweet Romance* series. He's a romantic at heart, with a passion for celebrating life, love, and the beautiful connections between humans and animals. His soulful stories capture the essence of opening oneself up to the possibilities that love can bring, and the magic that can unfold when we do.

If you're a fan of sweet, clean and wholesome, swoon-worthy romance stories that will leave you feeling uplifted and inspired, then his novels are a must-read.

Kerk is also the founder of *The Lexi's Legacy Foundation*, a coastal Georgia 501(c)(3) nonprofit organization committed to ending animal suffering. A portion of his books' proceeds are donated to the nonprofit and together with the support of his readers, the lives of hundreds of abused animals have been changed forever.

Join him on his mission in creating a more compassionate world for all living beings, one heartwarming story at a time.

Follow Kerk on social media and sign up for his mailing list at **kerkmurray.com** to stay updated on his latest releases and sneak peeks into his upcoming works.

amazon.com/stores/Kerk-Murray/author/B09C39NLYT

goodreads.com/author/show/21719388.Kerk_Murray

bookbub.com/profile/kerk-murray

instagram.com/kerkmurray

facebook.com/kerkwrites

tiktok.com/@kerkmurray